Essays in the Philosophy of Art

Essays in
the Philosophy
of Art

BY

R. G. COLLINGWOOD

EDITED, WITH AN INTRODUCTION

BY ALAN DONAGAN

Indiana University Press

BLOOMINGTON

CONTENTS

Introduction by Alan Donagan   ix

Ruskin's Philosophy   3

1 Ruskin not a Philosophical Writer   5
2 Ruskin's Attitude towards Philosophy   7
3 On the Philosophy of Non-Philosophers   9
4 Logicism and Historicism   12
5 Ruskin as Historicist   17
6 The Anti-Historicism of Ruskin's Contemporaries   24
7 The Unity of the Spirit: Corollaries and Illustrations   30
8 Ruskin and Browning   37
9 Conclusion   40

Outlines of a Philosophy of Art   43

Author's Preface   45

1 The General Nature of Art
    1 The Problem   47
    2 Art in its Generic Nature   49
    3 Art in its Specific Nature: Theoretically, as Imagination   52
    4 The Primitiveness of Art   55

5   Art in its Specific Nature: Practically,
      as the Pursuit of Beauty   60

6   The Monadism of Art   65

7   Art in its Specific Nature: Emotionally,
      as the Enjoyment of Beauty   68

2   *The Forms of Beauty*

8   The Forms of Beauty   72

9   The Sublime   77

10 The Comic   79

11 The Beautiful   83

3   *The Beauty of Nature*

12 The Imaginary Object and the Real Object   89

13 Inspiration   92

14 Nature   94

15 The Beauty of Nature   97

16 The Forms of Natural Beauty   101

4   *The Work of Art*

17 The Birth of Art   112

18 The Work of Art in its Immaturity   115

19 Formal Art   119

20 Naturalistic Art   121

21 Imaginative Art   125

5   *The Life of Art*

22 The Work of Art and the Life of Art   128

23 Genius and Taste: The Classics   131

24 The Revolt against the Classics   132

25 The Life of Art in its Freedom   135

6   *Art and the Life of the Spirit*

26 The Life of the Spirit: Art and Religion   137

27 Science, History, Philosophy   141

CONTENTS

28   The Unity of the Spiritual Life   144

29   The Mortality and Immortality of Art   146

30   Art and its History   148

Suggestions for Further Study   153

Plato's Philosophy of Art   155

The Place of Art in Education   185

Form and Content in Art   209

The spelling, capitalization, and punctuation of the original publication has been in every case preserved, save for the correction of evident misprints and for the bringing of quotation conventions into uniformity. For purposes of reference, the original pagination is given in parentheses at the top of the left-hand pages throughout the book.

INTRODUCTION

R. G. COLLINGWOOD (1889-1943) is generally acknowledged to have contributed more to the philosophy of art
and the philosophy of history than any other British
philosopher of his time. His *Principles of Art* (1938)
and *Idea of History* (1946) are readily obtainable and
widely studied. Yet, despite his beautiful and vigorous
prose style, neither of these important books is fully intelligible by itself. You must go to *The New Leviathan*
(1942) if you would understand the philosophy of mind
that he partly developed in *The Principles of Art*; and
you will probably misinterpret the methodology of *The
Idea of History* if you neglect his impassioned but revealing *Autobiography* (1939).

In order fully to master Collingwood's philosophy of
art you must go even farther afield: to the writings, all of
them published in the years from 1922 to 1929, which
are reprinted in this book. Except for the passages on
art in his general philosophical works, for reviews, and
for a chapter on "Aesthetic" contributed to a collabora-
tive work, *The Mind*, edited by R. J. S. McDowall, they
include everything Collingwood wrote about aesthetics
before *The Principles of Art*. In them, you can follow
his thought in the process of formation.

In the earliest of them, *Ruskin's Philosophy*, the philosopher whom Collingwood praised with least reserve

was Hegel. His debt to Hegel is obvious in the dialectical structure of the second and third chapters of *Outlines of a Philosophy of Art*. It is also obvious, although less directly, in its sixth chapter, which summarizes the "phenomenology of mind" which Collingwood had elaborated a year before in *Speculum Mentis*. According to that phenomenology, art is the first of the five activities of the whole human spirit: the others are, in order, religion, science, history, and philosophy. They constitute a scale of forms, in which the more advanced both contain and correct the more primitive. Art, the most primitive of the five, is purely imaginative, and interested only in its internal coherence. Most works of art have meaning, but not as such: as works of art they are windowless monads which do not even know that they are windowless. Religion, which is also imaginative, includes art: but it transcends art in dogmatically affirming that its imagery conveys truth. In turn, religion requires a higher activity to transcend it, because it cannot comprehend that it conveys truth only metaphorically, and so cannot inquire what that truth is. It would be superfluous to pursue the dialectic by which Collingwood elucidates the higher phases of mental life: science, history, and philosophy. Every phase, he declared, is "a nisus towards self-consciousness," which is finally fulfilled in philosophical insight.

This impressive scheme has paradoxical consequences for art which Collingwood did not try to conceal. If artists as artists are unaware of what their work means, then it follows, as he conceded in *Speculum Mentis*, that they cannot do well even as artists unless "they are more than artists" (p. 102). He expressed the same paradox in the *Outlines*, when he wrote that "we may value art for what

it says, because what it says is beautiful; or for what it)
means, because what it means, but does not say, is true")
(p. 147).[1] Since he did not deny that the meaning of a work
of art partly determines its value, he could not escape the
conclusion that its value partly lies outside itself: "the
value of art as a form of experience," he confessed, "is . . . ⟩
its self-transcendence" (*Speculum Mentis,* p. 90). Alas, his ⟩
account in the *Outlines* of the self-transcendence of art
was disastrous.

As art actually exists [he wrote] it exists not in . . . isolation,
but in the closest union with thought [i.e. the four higher
phases of mental life]; what has by thought been grasped becomes expressive, because immediate, in the form of art, *and
thus every . . . other phase of the spiritual life passes into art,*
there to be focused into a luminous point *from which it can
reissue into the explicitness of thought* (p. 148, my italics).

Collingwood's position here is, on the one hand, that
you can only "grasp," or be aware of, what is "immediate"
or "luminous," i.e. art; and, on the other hand, that you
cannot express what you mean without mediacy, i.e.
thought. From this the absurdity follows that nobody can
become aware of what he thinks. Even if a thought should
"pass into" art (becoming an object of awareness, but ceasing to say what it means), and then "reissue" into thought
(coming again to say what it means, but ceasing to be
an object of awareness), it would not at any point become an awareness of a thought. In the same way, if a
surface is painted black all over, and then white all over,
it does not at any time become black *and* white all over.

To escape this absurdity Collingwood found it necessary to modify his position slightly but profoundly.

1. This reference and all other references to works included in this
volume are to the pagination of the text that follows.

Whereas in the *Outlines* he had held that art, or imagination, always exists "in the closest union with thought," which transcends it, in *The Principles of Art* he recognized that imagination is a necessary element in every act of thought. To think is not to transcend imagination, but to put imagination to work in a specific way.

Although the dialectical phenomenology in the *Outlines*, like an unwieldy suit of armour, may once have afforded protection against adversaries long forgotten, it now only conceals the shape of Collingwood's thought. Its place in his philosophy of art, as he himself had written of a Lockean doctrine in Ruskin's *Modern Painters*, "is not structural but ornamental." Stripped of ornamentation, Collingwood's aesthetic can be seen to have owed little to Hegel, and almost everything to Ruskin and Croce.

As the first chapter of his *Autobiography* shows, Collingwood was bred from childhood in the practice of art as Ruskin conceived it. He had himself received the training he prescribes in his essay "Art in Education"; and he received it at home, from his father, W. G. Collingwood, Ruskin's disciple, friend, and biographer. What above all Collingwood owed to Ruskin's influence was the conviction that in all its manifestations each human mind is a unity. In *Ruskin's Philosophy*, he acknowledged his debt for the principle; and he also followed Ruskin in some of his applications of it. For example, when he wrote that a painter "paints in order to see" (*Outlines*, p. 129), and described "drawing, painting and modelling" as "the training of the eye" ("Art in Education," p. 202), he was repeating Ruskin's lesson in *Oxford Lectures on Art* that the power to draw is inseparable from the power to see. Ruskin, indeed, went further, holding "fine technical work" to be a proof of "every other good power."[2] Again, when Collingwood wrote that "if we are to recover the artistic sanity of the Greeks and the Middle Ages and the Renaissance, we must first recover the conviction that nothing can be beautifully made unless it is efficiently made, nothing efficiently made unless it is beautifully made" ("Art in Education," p. 194), he was repeating another of Ruskin's dicta: "from highest to lowest, health of art has first depended on reference to industrial use" (*Oxford Lectures*, IV § 117, p. 108).

Collingwood nevertheless conceded that on one point Ruskin had misapplied his principle. In *Two Paths* Ruskin had written that "the period in which any given people reach their highest power in art is precisely that in which they appear to sign the warrant of their own ruin . . ." (*Ruskin's Philosophy*, p. 35). Attributing public ruin to moral decay, he had gone on to infer that art flourishes when morality withers, which contradicts his inference from the principle of the unity of the human mind that "the manual arts are as accurate exponents of ethical state, as other modes of expression; first, with absolute precision, of that of the workman; and then with precision, disguised by many distorting influences, of that of the nation to which it belongs" (*Oxford Lectures*, III § 71, pp. 77-8).

Ruskin twice attempted, but without success, to escape this contradiction. First, he denied that an art which

---

2. *Oxford Lectures on Art* III, §74; in *The Works of John Ruskin*, ed. E. T. Cook and Alexander Wedderburn (London, 1905) vol. xx, p. 80. Collingwood's "Art in Education" is a free variation on Ruskin's argument in the first half of his fourth *Oxford Lecture*, that art "exists rightly only when it is the means of knowledge, or the grace of agency for life" (*ibid.* p. 96).

flourishes when morality decays can be a true art, on the ground that it is not naturalistic. But the art of Michelangelo and Tintoretto was naturalistic. Later, he explained that "the great art-periods of the past were fatal to national life because art has always been in the service of a rich and proud nobility, careless of the misery in which its less fortunate neighbours lay" (*Ruskin's Philosophy,* p. 36). This explanation implies of Tintoretto's art either that it is proud and callous, which Ruskin did not think, or that its quality is not an exponent of the morality of Tintoretto's nation, which contradicts Ruskin's hypothesis.

Collingwood found an explanation of the impermanence of artistic styles in Browning's line, "What's come to perfection perishes." "[T]he perfection of any one artistic style . . . lays a dilemma before the human spirit: either . . . become merely imitative, or else launch out into the void, feeling for a new style . . . and acquiescing in the death of the old" (*ibid.* pp. 37-38). But why should not art become merely imitative? In answering this question Collingwood could get no help from Ruskin or Browning. He had to look beyond them, to Croce.

Collingwood's relations with Croce were very close. He translated into English two of Croce's books (the first of them in 1913), and two articles, one of them the important "Aesthetic" for the *Encyclopaedia Britannica* (14th ed.). In a letter to Croce written in 1921 Collingwood referred to himself as "a friend and disciple of your philosophy," and Croce's influence on his philosophy of art grew with the years. Of *The Principles of Art* (1938), he was to write to Croce that "the doctrine taught in it is in all essentials your own." Yet, even allowing for grateful hyperbole, he could not have written so about his earlier *Outlines.* He did, indeed, acknowledge in his Preface

that the "general conception" of art expounded in the
Outlines was "already familiar from the works of Coleridge, Croce, and many others" (p. 45). But in elaborating
that general conception he diverged considerably from
Croce.

The *Outlines* follows Croce in defining art generically
as a mental activity, and specifically as imaginative. It
also follows Croce in describing imagination as unconcerned with the reality or unreality of the objects it
creates. Furthermore, in it Collingwood adopted Croce's
distinction between sensation and imagination: sensation yields only "impressions," which fall short of full
awareness; it is imagination that raises sense-impressions
to the level of consciousness, creating what Croce called
"intuitions." Although Collingwood eschewed Croce's
terminology, he clearly drew Croce's distinction in passages like the following. "[A] painter paints . . . in order to
see. . . . A person who does not draw has only a dim and
vague feeling of the look of things, and at no single point
has he a clear or accurate grasp of their appearance. . . .
Similarly, the practice of music is a sharpening of our
discrimination with regard to the pitch, intensity, quality
and inter-relations of sounds; the drama and the novel
perform the same function with regard to human nature"
(p. 129). It may be observed that, in the final sentence of
this passage, Collingwood implicitly extended the province of art to every level of consciousness: "human nature" is not an object of sensation.

In reformulating Croce's analysis of imagination, Collingwood gave it a Ruskinian tincture. Although Croce
maintained that every imaginative creation has a physical
counterpart, he also maintained that properly a work of
art exists in the mind, its physical counterpart being no
more than an "externalization" produced, not by art, but

by "technique."[3] Croce's proposition that art is not the
exercise of a technique was accepted by Collingwood
(*Outlines*, p. 118); nor is it, taken by itself, inconsistent
with Collingwood's Ruskinian proposition that technique, while primarily a matter of muscular control, is
"secondarily . . . a training not of the muscles but of the
eye and ear, or, more precisely, of the imagination . . ."
(*Outlines*, p. 117). Croce did not deny that you cannot
imagine visually unless you learn to draw; indeed, he
expressly stated that you do not imagine clearly what a
thing looks like unless you can draw it.[4] But he did not
emphasize it. Following Ruskin, Collingwood did.

The definition of art as imaginative enabled Collingwood to answer the question, "Why should art not be
merely imitative?" If art is imaginative, it is the activity
by which we become conscious of our impressions; but
our impressions are not those of previous generations.
"The transformations which art undergoes in the course
of its history are the expression not of a self-contained life
of art . . . , but of the life of the spirit as a whole" (*Outlines*, p. 151). As conditions of life change art must
change; and the art of the past can only be appreciated
by an effort of historical imagination (*ibid*. p. 150).[5]

Since he held that every mental activity has a conative
or "practical" and an emotional side, as well as a cognitive one, Collingwood could not accept as complete the
definition of art as imagination, which refers only to its

3. Croce's theory of externalization and its connexion with technique
is elucidated in G. N. G. Orsini, *Benedetto Croce: Philosopher of Art and
Literary Critic* (Carbondale, 1961). pp. 89-95.

4. B. Croce, *Aesthetic*, tr. Douglas Ainslie (London, 1922), p. 11.

5. Collingwood also inferred that "art, as art, has no history . . . there
is only the history of humanity" (*Outlines*, p. 151). In *The Idea of
History* (Oxford, 1946), pp. 313-4, he revised this extreme view, conced-
ing that "there is . . . a history of art," but denying that there is a "history
of artistic problems."

cognitive side. A complete definition must take account of its practical and emotional sides.

Practically, Collingwood maintained, art attempts to achieve beauty; and emotionally, it is the enjoyment of beauty, so far as beauty is achieved. And, repudiating the notion that any activity of mind can properly be judged by a criterion outside itself, he went on to conclude that beauty, as the criterion by which art is practically judged, must be defined in terms of art itself, i.e. of imagination. He therefore defined it as "the unity or coherence of the imaginary object" (*Outlines*, pp. 62-63).

This definition can hardly fail to appear circular. Art, i.e. imagination, attempts to achieve beauty, i.e. the unity or coherence possessed by whatever is imagined. But what unity or coherence is that? You may even be tempted to close the book in disgust when you find Collingwood impeccably deducing that "it is impossible to imagine anything that is not beautiful," and that "all ugliness, so far as it does actually exist, is not the ugliness of an object imagined but the ugliness of an object not imagined" (*Outlines*, pp. 61, 62). Attempting to achieve beauty is attempting to imagine well: but in trying to imagine well, what are we trying to achieve?

Two answers to this question may be dismissed at once. It will not do to say that we are simply trying to achieve clear awareness. It is true that Collingwood held that imagination is the activity by which we become aware of things; but we do not try to become aware of anything and everything. Of what does an artist try to become aware? Nor will it do to say that he tries to become aware of what it is useful to be aware of. Even if in education the aim of art is to enable a child to be practically efficient when he grows up, that aim is external to art. It is not the function of art *in itself*. What is that function?

Croce answered his question in a paper of 1908, which was included as an appendix to Ainslie's 1909 English translation of *Aesthetic*, and in *Problemi di Estetica* (1910). Although it is in the last degree improbable that Collingwood had not read these works, they left little or no mark on his *Outlines*. But in "Form and Content in Art" the latest of the papers in this collection, he showed signs of assimilating their teaching; and when he wrote *The Principles of Art* he had wholly done so.

Briefly, Croce argued that art is the attempt to express emotion. In his terminology, artistic intuition is "lyrical."[6] As Croce wrote: "what confers coherence and unity upon the intuition is emotion . . . an intuition is truly such when it represents an emotion, and can rise only from it and above it. . . . Not the idea, but the emotion is what confers upon art the ethereal lightness of the symbol: a longing enclosed within the circumference of an image: that is art. . . ."[7] Croce would have rejected as absurd the question, "Why does the artist try to express his emotion?" By its very nature, emotion strives towards expression.

In "Form and Content in Art" Collingwood identified the content of art with what he called its "romantic element," to which he variously referred as "the connexions that bind art to the rest of life" (p. 227), "emotion," "consciousness of a sincere interest," and "conviction" pp. 229ff.). And he argued that a work of art can be created only when this romantic element goes together with a "classical element," which he identified with "the artist's formal or formative power" (p. 226). Despite his carelessly anti-Crocean use of the word "technique," what in this paper he described as the formal or classical ele-

---

6. Croce's theory is admirably expounded in Orsini, *op. cit.*, ch. 3.
7. Quoted and translated by Orsini, *op. cit.*, p. 54.

ment in art clearly corresponds to what Croce called "intuition," and what he described as the romantic element in art corresponds to what Croce called its "lyrical" character. The following remarks from the penultimate paragraph of Collingwood's essay anticipate the thought and even the phrasing of his later, fully Crocean, doctrine in *The Principles of Art*, pp. 109-10. "[U]ntil he has learnt to speak, [the artist] has nothing to say. He may have feelings working within him, but they are only obscure emotional perturbations, and do not take the shape of . . . a conviction . . . brought clearly before himself."

Why did not Collingwood from the first embrace the conception of art as the expression of emotion? Any answer must be conjectural. But it is significant that the *Outlines* diverges most strikingly from Croce's *Aesthetic* in giving a central place to the concept of beauty. In this he followed Ruskin and the German idealists. It is true that by defining beauty in terms of a Crocean concept of imagination, he emptied it of the content it had for them. But was he aware of this? Echoing Hobbes, I make bold to submit that the theory of beauty in the *Outlines* is the ghost of the Ruskinian conception sitting crowned upon the grave thereof. In "Form and Content in Art" Collingwood made no use of the concept of beauty; and in *The Principles of Art* he argued that "aesthetic theory is the theory not of beauty but of art" (p. 41), and that the theory of beauty belongs with the theory of love.

The paper on "Plato's Philosophy of Art" is a contribution rather to the study of Plato than to the philosophy of art. As such it has great intrinsic interest. Readers should, however, be warned that Collingwood later repudiated its attribution to Plato of the doctrine that all art is mimetic (i.e. imitative or representative): "If any one," he wrote, "will read the first half of [*Republic*]

Book x with an unprejudiced eye, he will see that Plato never tells his reader . . . that he regards poetry in general as representative" (*Principles of Art*, p. 48; cf. p. 46 *n.*).

ALAN DONAGAN

Bloomington, Indiana

Essays in the Philosophy of Art

Ruskin's Philosophy

1   *RUSKIN NOT A*
PHILOSOPHICAL WRITER

To many of you, and those not the least acquainted with the works of Ruskin, the title of my address must seem a paradox. These works, taken as a whole, form an encyclopaedia in which painting, architecture and poetry stand side by side with history, geography and geology, politics and economics, studies in bird-flight and flower-growth, in perspective and prosody. Each of these subjects in turn, and many others, Ruskin made his own and seldom failed to illuminate with fresh observation. The time is long past when he could be regarded as an art-critic who strayed beyond his province to dabble in political economy, and past no less, I hope and believe, is the time when he could be regarded as a social reformer who wasted his youth in art-criticism. To-day we must look at Ruskin as a whole or not at all.

But, looking at him as a whole, and considering what I have called the encyclopaedia of his works, we find that

Ruskin's Philosophy: An Address delivered at the Ruskin Centenary Conference, Coniston, August 8th, 1919. Kendal, England: Titus Wilson & Son, 1922.

it is an encyclopaedia with a gap. All the arts and almost all the sciences are passed in review; but there is no treatise, however small, on philosophy. The apparent exceptions to this rule only serve to prove it. In the second volume of *Modern Painters* an attempt is made to place the new art-criticism on a philosophical basis, and a theory of art is elaborated, based on a theory of the human mind. It is quite clear to any careful reader that the author, fresh from his Oxford readings in Locke and the Scottish psychologists, felt called upon by the importance of the occasion to assume the philosopher's gown, and did so with youthful solemnity. But the doctrine of the Theoretic Faculty is not Ruskin's philosophy of art; its existence is due to influences from which he had not yet shaken himself free; and its place in *Modern Painters* is not structural but ornamental. Those writers who have quoted it as Ruskin's contribution to aesthetics[1] have only succeeded in demonstrating their ignorance of his work as a whole.

Another exception that proves the rule is the little paper read before the Metaphysical Society in 1871 and entitled *"The Range of Intellectual Conception proportioned to the Rank in Animated Life" (On The Old Road; Works, 34, 107-111).* Here, certainly, is an attempt at a philosophical essay, but a strikingly unsuccessful one; the author has evidently been asked to write a paper for the Metaphysical Society, has cudgelled his brains for something to say, and has found nothing.

With these exceptions, each due to external and rather unsympathetic influence, and each an entire failure, Ruskin never wrote a philosophical work at all; for such a book as *Ethics of the Dust* is not philosophy but morals, a quite different thing. We may say, therefore, that

1. E.g. Croce, *Estetica*, ed. 4, 1912; pp. 447-448.

though he wrote books about everything else he never wrote one on philosophy.

2 RUSKIN'S ATTITUDE TOWARDS PHILOSOPHY

Further, you doubtless recall passages in which he refers to philosophy and philosophers; and, if so, you will remember that the tone of these references is almost always hostile and contemptuous. I could quote you a dozen such passages; but perhaps the most instructive is that in the third volume of *Modern Painters* (*Works*, 5, 333-334) where he contrasts seers and thinkers to the great disadvantage of the latter: laying down that "metaphysicians and philosophers are, on the whole, the greatest troubles the world has got to deal with." The metaphysician, it appears, is a greater plague to mankind than even the tyrant or the idler; for while these may in certain circumstances be a blessing in disguise, the metaphysician never does anything except clog with his cobwebs the fine wheels of the world's business.

The reason why this passage is valuable is that Ruskin has appended a footnote in the following terms.

"Observe, I do not speak thus of metaphysics because I have no pleasure in them. When I speak contemptuously of philology, it may be answered me that I am a bad scholar; but I cannot be so answered touching metaphysics, for everyone conversant with such subjects may see that I have strong inclination that way, which would, indeed, have led me far astray, long ago, if I had not learned also some use of my hands, eyes, and feet."

This passage, together with others like it, shows us

three things: first, that Ruskin had read a certain amount of philosophy; second, that he felt a strong natural bent in the direction of that study; and third, that he nevertheless looked upon philosophy as a futile and dangerous pursuit, which it was his duty to avoid.

This, then, is the paradox to which I referred at the outset: that Ruskin not only never wrote on philosophy, but actually avoided it, with a deliberation due not to indifference but to reasoned hostility. And yet I am addressing you on the subject of Ruskin's philosophy.

To speak of his philosophical studies is clearly not enough. We know that at Oxford he read the old-fashioned logic, and disliked it; some Aristotle, partly with great admiration and partly with equal annoyance; some Plato; and some of the moderns—Bacon, Locke, Dugald Stewart and Thomas Brown.[2] Later, we find him reading German metaphysics, and coming to the conclusion that the Germans were very bad metaphysicians;[3] but he never tackled the greater German idealists, except for one dubious attempt—instigated no doubt by Carlyle—to read Fichte,[4] out of whom he got nothing. Plato alone he read and re-read, loved and revered, to the end of his life.

All these facts would seem to suggest that Ruskin did indeed read a little philosophy, just as he read a little of everything else; that he was "good at it" in his undergraduate days, just as he was good at mathematics; but that it was a study he never pursued seriously. He never mastered the first rudiments of modern idealism; he

2. Collingwood, *Life*, I., 97.

3. Letter to Carlyle; Collingwood, *Life*, I., 195; not reprinted in *Works*. In point of fact what Ruskin was sampling was very second-rate stuff and quite out of date at the time.

4. The evidence is a letter to Dr. John Brown in 1880; *Works*, 37, 318. It does not prove that he had actually read any Fichte; he may be referring to phrases and ideas learnt in conversation from Carlyle, who was a follower of Fichte.

never really understood Aristotle; he read Plato for his style, his temperament, and his social and political ideas, but not for his metaphysics. In short, Ruskin was no philosopher; he had not the necessary qualifications; and his studies in modern philosophy were too cursory and too ill-directed to entitle him to an opinion on its merits.

All this is true: yet I hope to show you that in devoting one entire meeting at this conference to Ruskin's philosophy we shall not be wasting our time. I am speaking not about his attitude to philosophy, not about his acquaintance with philosophy, but about his philosophy; and to have a philosophy is a very different thing from reading philosophy or being a philosopher. Indeed, one might venture to say that philosophers are the people who least of all have a philosophy of their own. Shoemakers' children, they say, go ill-shod; and a man who is always taking his watch to pieces, to see how it works, is not the best man to tell you the time.

3 ON THE PHILOSOPHY OF NON-PHILOSOPHERS

When I speak of a man's philosophy, I mean something of this sort. I see a man living a long and busy life; I see him doing a large number of different things, or writing a large number of different books. And I ask myself, do these actions, or these books, hang together? Is there any central thread on which they are all strung? Is there any reason why the man who wrote this book should have gone on to write that one, or is it pure chance? Is there anything like a constant purpose, or a consistent point of view, running through all the man's work?

Now if you ask these questions about a particular man, you will generally find that there are certain central principles which the man takes as fundamental and incontrovertible, which he assumes as true in all his thinking and acting. These principles form, as it were, the nucleus of his whole mental life: they are the centre from which all his activities radiate. You may think of them as a kind of ring of solid thought—something infinitely tough and hard and resistent[5]—to which everything the man does is attached. The ring is formed of a number of different ideas or principles, welded together by some force of mutual cohesion.

This ring of thought—this nucleus of the individual mind—is what I mean by a man's philosophy. Everyone has it, whether he is a philosopher or not: and a man is a great man or a little, a valuable man or a worthless, largely according as this ring is strong or weak in structure, good or bad in material. The acts and decisions which shape a man's life are suspended from this ring of principles; and if the ring is weak a heavy load will snap it; the man's character, as we say, fails to stand the strain and we brand him henceforward as untrustworthy. Or again, if the principles of which the ring is composed are unsound and untrue, then the judgments and actions which issue from them are wrong and mistaken, and we call the man a bad or foolish man.

This central core of convictions, which is the nucleus and basis of the whole life, exists in each one of us, and in that sense every one of us has a philosophy. But for the most part we do not know that we possess it: still less do we know what are the convictions which constitute it. The fact seems to be that a man's deepest convictions are

5. I do not mean by this to imply that they never change. Often they are in motion, but a motion seldom perceptible by the naked eye.

precisely those which he never puts into words. Everything which he says and does is based upon his grasp of these convictions; but just because his grasp of them is so complete, so unquestioning, he never finds it necessary to express them at all. If you expressed them for him, he would say, "why waste time in saying that there is a sun in the sky and earth under my feet? Why not get on and say something that matters—something I didn't know before?"

It may seem strange that our deepest and most important convictions should habitually go unexpressed. But this is still stranger, that we are often quite mistaken as to what these convictions are. If you ask a man to state his fundamental beliefs, and then carefully watch his actions and sayings, you will generally find that these are based on a set of beliefs quite different from the ones which he has stated. So the attempt to discover a man's philosophy often reveals facts very startling to the man himself—facts which he will regard less as truisms than as paradoxes.

Now it is this attempt to discover what people's philosophy is that marks the philosopher. Much as everybody has a brain, but only the anatomist sets himself to discover what it looks like and how it works, so everybody has a philosophy, but only the philosopher makes it his business to probe into the mind and lay bare that recess in which the ultimate beliefs lie hidden.

A great man like Ruskin, then, necessarily has not only a philosophy but an important and interesting philosophy; but, not being a philosopher, Ruskin did not dissect his own mind to find out what his philosophy was. This can only be done by examining his works and finding what general philosophical principles underlie them; and for this purpose it is necessary to be guided not by the language of this or that isolated passage, but by the attitude, the frame of mind, the intellectual merits and defects, exemplified in his work as a whole. Some such analysis as this I shall try to lay before you; but by way of preface I must begin by reminding you of the chief philosophical ideas that were in the air during the period —say 1820 to 1850—when Ruskin's mind was reaching maturity.

4 *LOGICISM AND HISTORICISM*

One of the most remarkable facts about the history of thought in the middle nineteenth century is the conflict between two methods of thinking which I shall call the Logical[6] and the Historical. The logical method of thinking proceeds on the assumption that every individual fact is an instance of some eternal and unchanging principle, some law to which time makes no difference; and that the general law is more important, more valuable to know, more real, than the particular fact which is a mere instance of it—no better and no worse than countless other instances. The aim of knowledge, therefore, must always be the discovery of these general laws; and the same laws, when discovered, serve as the foundation for further knowledge and for practical activities. The task of the scientist is to explain facts, and to explain a fact is to show what law it exemplifies. The task of the statesman is so to govern his country that its national life shall

6. I use the term, throughout, with reference to that Logic which dominated thought between the time of Aristotle and that of Kant; but without prejudging the question whether this is a true logic— *i.e.* a true description of thinking.

so far as possible obey and exemplify the eternal principles of justice and the natural rights of man.

This type of thought has certain practical consequences, easy to recognize in whatever sphere of life they occur. First, a kind of contempt for facts—facts of science, of history, of human nature, of general experience. The person who, on being told that his theory was at variance with the facts, replied *tant pis pour les faits*, was a philosopher of this school. Secondly, a habitual intolerance. If you believe that there are such things as eternal and natural rights of man, and that your political system is based on these rights, you naturally conclude that any different political system must be utterly immoral and worthless. If you believe in an abstract and perfect ideal beauty—a *beau idéal* in the old-fashioned French terminology—and intend your own style in art to express this ideal, you cannot possibly take a real interest in other styles. Thirdly, a tendency towards monotony and rigidity in all kinds of mental work; a tendency to repeat yourself or even to set up repetition as an admirable thing and one to be encouraged, and to avoid and decry all departure from the paved highway of rule and precedent.

You may see these qualities conspicuous in all sides of human activity during the seventeenth and eighteenth centuries, that "age of rationalism" in which logical thinking was universally in fashion. The political theorists of the time all believed in some system of eternal and immutable rights, from which political institutions drew their validity; in this article of faith, partisans of the divine right of kings were at one with the advocates of the rights of man. The moralists (the real moralists, I mean) believed in a moral law which knew no exception and admitted no taint of interest or expediency; the art-

critics, in the "unities" of the stage and in a rigid ad-
herence to classical forms. And if you wish to see how
these ideas influenced the practical work of painters and
writers, you have only to look through the plates in
Claude's *Liber Veritatis,* and see how almost every one is
composed in the same way out of the same materials—a
lump of trees in the middle, another lump of trees half-
seen on one side, a cluster of Corinthian columns half-
seen on the other; in between, a view of distant mountains. Or examine the rhymed couplets of Pope, all cast
in the same mould and often so much alike that if you
shuffled them and brought them out in a different order,
nobody who did not know the poem by heart could tell.
Such examples fairly illustrate the effect on art of this
logical type of thinking.

The historical habit of mind is in every way a complete
contrast. Where the logical mind looks for general laws,
the historical mind looks for individual facts, and it explains these facts by appealing not to laws but to other
facts. When challenged for an explanation, it asks, not
"what general law does this fact illustrate?" but, "in
what particular circumstances did it arise?" Employed
in the pursuit of art, it asks, not "what are the rules for
composing a picture?" but, what is the most effective way
of composing this particular picture?" Faced with the
problems of political life, it tries not so much to determine the natural rights of man as to get at the rights and
wrongs of this particular war, controversy or proposal.

This type of thought, like the other, has definite and
easily recognised consequences. It is the reverse of everything that we mean by the word doctrinaire. It prefers
facts to theories, and will not theorise at all—if it can be
helped—till it can cast its net wide enough to take in all
the facts that can be discovered. Hence its natural inclina-

tion is always toward tolerance; for it respects facts to such an extent as to suppose that nothing can ever have existed unless it had something to say for itself. This induces a broad outlook and a readiness to study, not without sympathy, ideals which differ widely from one's own. A mind of this cast is supple, both in theory and in practice, where the other is rigid, and aims at freedom and variety where the other aims at uniform and unquestioning obedience to precept and precedent.

This historical habit of thought was coming into existence[7] in the early nineteenth century, and its rise is shown in a number of different ways. First, a growing interest in the architecture, art, politics, poetry, and religion of the Middle Ages, a period whose ideals the eighteenth century had regarded with mere abhorrence. Secondly, a growing freedom with regard to art-forms. Pope believed that there was one eternally perfect metre, and wrote in it always. Browning, a typical son of the nineteenth century, believed that every poem must evolve its own metre out of its own inner necessity. And this difference in style between the two poets is intimately connected with the fact that Pope, living in an age of logic and seeing philosophy in terms of logic, wrote his philosophy of human life in the form of an abstract, generalised *Essay on Man*, while Browning, living in a historical age and thinking of philosophy in terms of history, wrote his in the form of a historical study—the life of Sordello. Thirdly, a growing scepticism with regard to the permanence of political structures. It was no accident that the generation which saw the rise of the historical type of thought was also essentially the age of revolutions; or that the revolutionary socialism of to-day can trace a direct descent from the greatest of historical philosophers.

7. Its roots, of course, may be traced earlier.

In calling these two types of thought the logical and the historical respectively I do not mean to imply that the first has no dealings with history nor the second with logic. There were historians in the seventeenth and eighteenth centuries; but their notion of what history ought to be was a trivial and elementary thing compared with the vast development of historical knowledge and historical method which took place in the nineteenth century. And again, there were plenty of great logicians in the nineteenth century; but their logic was a very different thing from that of their predecessors. The logic which was still, in the seventeenth and eighteenth centuries, the mistress and norm of all science was the old scholastic logic of formal correctness, consistency, clarity and definiteness in thinking; and the habit of mind which I call logicism consists in the application of this ideal to all forms of mental activity.

Now it seems to be the fact that this ideal, conscientiously followed, makes a true understanding of history impossible. To deal with history the logical mind must first distort it, as history certainly was distorted by an age which blindly adored the ancient world and blindly detested the Middle Ages, instead of forming— as anyone with a sound historical sense would do—a cool judgment on the merits and defects of each. No one can be a true historian till he realises that truth is many-sided and not to be attained by the pursuit of logical consistency; till he has discovered that he cannot be both a historian and, in the old sense of the word, a logician. But this very fact led to the rejection of the old logic, and the growth of a new logic whose whole being was rooted in history; so that just as logicism produced its own school of history, historicism created for itself a logic.

The conflict between these two types of thought was

by no means evenly matched. By the time Ruskin began to write, a consistent logicism no longer existed; it had everywhere been modified by the encroachments of a growing interest in the past; and the change had even begun to affect the philosophers. Thus the Kantian, Sir William Hamilton, was chiefly celebrated for his researches into the history of philosophy.

Historicism was already beginning to show itself as the philosophy of the future. The teaching in which it was systematically expressed, that of Hegel, superseded all previous philosophies when once it was understood; and even while Hegel was still regarded as unintelligible, the movement of thought which he represented was showing its power and gathering weight at the expense of its rival. Of this historical movement Ruskin was a whole-hearted adherent, and every detail of his work is coloured and influenced by the fact. In a quite real sense he was a Hegelian; not that he ever read Hegel,[8] or knew anything about him, but that he had the same outlook on the world, the same instinctive attitude towards reality, which made Hegel rewrite logic in terms of history.

5 RUSKIN AS HISTORICIST

This historicism or Hegelism of Ruskin has a whole cycle of unmistakable consequences. The first which I will ask you to consider, because I believe it to be in his case the most important, is the belief in the unity or solidarity

8. That he did not is as certain as negative evidence can make anything. He names him once, in the Metaphysical Society paper mentioned above, in 1871, when Hegel was just becoming known in England: but the reference shows that Ruskin only knew of him by hearsay, in connexion with something called the Absolute.

of the human spirit. Every reader must have noticed as characteristic of Ruskin that he never deals with the art of a particular person or nation without dragging in questions of morality, religion, politics, and so on. If he is asked what kind of training will produce good artists in this country, he will reply, "first of all you must remedy your social abuses: then you must set up a general high moral standard, and see that it is followed: and then, you will find, art will come of itself."

He deals with the past in exactly the same spirit. If there is something visibly good or bad in the art of a certain people at a certain date, he always assumes that there must have been exactly corresponding virtues and vices in their moral and political life. Now this kind of assumption betrays the presence of a definite theory of the human mind: the belief, namely, that each form of human activity springs not from a special faculty—an organ of the mind, so to speak—but from the whole nature of the person concerned: so that art is not the product of a special part of the mind called the "aesthetic faculty," nor morality the product of a special "moral faculty," but each alike is an expression of the whole self. Thus, if the ancient Greek was a man of a definite type and character, his art exhibited this character in one way, while his political systems and his religious beliefs exhibited the same character in another way, translated, as it were, into another language, but otherwise identical.

This principle—the unity and indivisibility of the spirit—Ruskin never questioned and never attempted to prove. He believed it instinctively; and it can be shown to proceed from the historical trend of his philosophy. The logical habit of mind finds ultimate reality in the shape of abstract general principles; it takes the historical fact of, say, ancient Greece, and analyses this fact into

abstract conceptions such as art, religion, political institutions and so on: and in so doing it feels that it is nearer
to reality than it was before. The historical habit of mind,
on the contrary, takes the historical fact of ancient Greece
as a whole, and regards this fact as ultimately real, or at
least, as real as anything short of the whole universe can
be—much more real than any abstraction such as "art"
or "religion." Thus, for the historical mind, Plato was a
Greek who happened to work at philosophy, and Phidias
a Greek who happened to work at sculpture. The important thing about them is not the medium in which
they worked but the fact that they both expressed the
Greek spirit: and therefore you get deeper into the mind
of Phidias by comparing him with Plato than by placing
him side by side with Rodin or Canova or Epstein. For
the logical mind, it is a mere accident that Plato and
Phidias were contemporaries. One belongs to the eternal
company of philosophers, the other to the equally eternal
and equally exclusive army of artists.

I shall illustrate later the way in which this principle—
the unity of the spirit—affects Ruskin's practical thinking; for the present I shall only ask you to observe that it
constitutes a breach with the whole trend of eighteenth-
century philosophy and a point of contact with Hegel, in
whose philosophy it was a cardinal axiom.

The second point in which Ruskin's thought shows a
historical tendency is the emphasis which he lays upon
historical causes. In the hands of a logically-minded
person, history becomes a mere succession of events, fact
following fact with little or no internal cohesion. To a
historically-minded person, on the contrary, history is a
drama, the unfolding of a plot in which each situation
leads necessarily to the next. Now nothing is more characteristic of Ruskin than his interest in the causes which

underlie history. Even in his earliest works, he is always pondering on the forces which cause national prosperity and decay; and it is a habit which remained with him throughout his life. Indeed, it became progressively stronger; and it was this interest which forced him to devote so much of his life to political and economic speculation. Here again he was definitely in agreement with Hegel, for whom every historical period carries within it the seeds of the next.

The third characteristic to which I want to call your attention is Ruskin's extreme tolerance. He was not tolerant in the sense of pretending to approve things which he felt to be wrong; but he was conspicuously tolerant in the sense of feeling the rightness and value of things which lay outside his own personal system of ideals.

As an example of this quality, consider his attitude towards the Middle Ages. He passionately admired and defended many things both in mediaeval life and in mediaeval art; but he had no intention of living like a baron or a monk, and painting pictures like the illuminations in a missal. He never for a moment wished to reinstate the Middle Ages,[9] or to copy their characteristic

9. *Two Paths*, III. In the middle of his fierce attack on the ugliness of modern industrial towns—a hopeless soil, he thinks, for a new school of decorative art—and his glowing picture of mediaeval Pisa, he suddenly breaks off:—

"I repeat, I do not ask you nor wish you to build a new Pisa for them. We don't want either the life or the decorations of the thirteenth century back again."

Compare the following passages, to which many might be added:—
Modern Painters, part iv., Ch. 15, 16, on the superiority of Scott to Dante.

Two Paths, II., 51. "If you glance over the map of Europe, you will find that where the manufactures are strongest, there art also is strongest."

And for pure, unsentimental and instinctive "modernism," this from the *Harbours of England*:—"I respect, in the merchant service, only those ships that carry coals, herrings, salt, timber, iron, and such other commodities, and have disagreeable odour and unwashed decks."

features; and if he had written a *News from Nowhere*, the London of his dreams would not have been built in the fashion of the fourteenth century.[10] He felt—and this is a matter on which his language is quite clear and definite —that the mediaeval ideals of art and life could never satisfy either him or his contemporaries; that they were wholly unsuitable for solving the problems of modern life; but that in spite of all this they contained much that was fine and noble and sincere, that they were deserving of admiration for what they accomplished in their day, and that the nineteenth century could learn much from their study.

Ruskin was a modernist. He cared intensely for science and progress, for political reform, for the advancement of knowledge and for new movements in art and letters. His own personal ideals were not the ideals of ancient Athens or mediaeval France or Renaissance Venice. His greatest work was written in praise of modern painters, and his favourite artist was a man who was too modern for all his contemporaries. If some fairy had asked him at what time in the world's history he would wish to have lived, he would have answered "To-day."

I lay stress on this because Ruskin's sympathy with Greek coin-designers, French cathedral-builders, and Italian fresco-painters is so spontaneous and complete that one is tempted to forget that it is only sympathy— only an imaginative, historical appreciation of a past which he recognised as past, which he admired but never worshipped, loved but never wished to restore. This is what I mean by tolerance: the ability to live one's own life and yet to admire and love people who live by the systems which one rejects.

This tolerance is the surest mark of the historical as

10. *Cf.* W. Morris, *News from Nowhere*, ch. iv.

opposed to the logical mind; and here, in this imaginative sympathy with the past, as opposed to idolatrous worship of one phase of the past, Ruskin's kinship with Hegel strikingly appears. For the Hegelian treatment of history depends on the principle that every historical phase has its own individual character, ideals and virtues, and that every phase alike should be an object of admiration, none of imitation.

I cannot refrain from citing a fourth characteristic of Ruskin's mind which even more strikingly, perhaps, shows his kinship with Hegel: I mean his attitude towards the logical problem of contradiction. Broadly speaking, there are two ways of looking at this problem. The old logic lays it down that of two contradictory propositions one must be false and the other true. To contradict yourself, on this view, is a sign of mental confusion: the wise man never contradicts himself. The alternative view starts from the axiom that there are two sides to every question, and that there is right on both sides; from this, the inference is drawn that truth is many-sided and that self-contradiction may easily be a mark not of weakness but of strength—not of confusion, but of a wide and comprehensive view which embraces much more truth than the one-sided consistency of the logicians.

Ruskin adopted the second of these views, and defended it explicitly in more than one well-known passage. You remember his discussion of the subject in the Cambridge Inaugural Lecture.[11]

"Perhaps some of my hearers this evening," he says, "may occasionally have heard it stated of me that I am rather apt to contradict myself. I hope I am exceedingly apt to do so. I never met with a question yet, of any importance, which did not need, for the right solution of

11. *Op. cit.* § 13: Works, 16, 187.

it, at least one positive and one negative answer, like an equation of the second degree. Mostly, matters of any consequence are three-sided, or four-sided, or polygonal; and the trotting round a polygon is severe work for people any way stiff in their opinions. For myself, I am never satisfied that I have handled a subject properly till I have contradicted myself at least three times."

This is no isolated statement of opinion.[12] Though he chose on this occasion to pass it off in a half-jocular form, he was perfectly serious about the principle. It was a firm and habitual belief with him—an instinctive belief, if you will—that by contradicting himself he got nearer the truth. It was an idea which he certainly did not get from Hegel; but I need hardly remind you that it is the very centre and core of Hegel's whole philosophy; which may indeed be described as a sustained attempt to live up to the maxim that in every conflict or dispute there is right on both sides. Both in Hegel's case and in Ruskin's, the recognition of this principle is associated with a sympathetic understanding of history; and, as we have already seen, the one is hardly possible without the other. The history of a struggle—and all history is the history of struggles—cannot be written by a man who believes that one party must have been simply right and the other simply wrong.

12. It is intimately connected with Ruskin's habitual procedure of uniting two apparently incompatible qualities in order to define the highest ideals. The best example, but only one of very many, is the long discourse in *The Nature of Gothic* (*Stones of Venice*, vol. II., ch. 6, §§ 41-49) on the text that art is divided into the art of facts (naturalistic) and the art of design (decorative). A writer of the eighteenth-century turn of mind would have gone on to ask "which of these is the right ideal for art? To which class does the best art belong?" Ruskin at once answers, "the best art is the union of both." § 44: "Most men have been made capable of giving one or the other, but not both: only one or two, the very highest, can give both." To define perfection in terms of a synthesis of opposites is one of Ruskin's most obvious and most Hegelian characteristics.

It is not my intention to defend in detail the use which Ruskin made of this idea. He often contradicted himself in mere petulance or carelessness; often he was driven to it by the excessive one-sidedness of something he had already said. His appeal to the polygonal character of truth covers a multitude of sins that ought never to have been committed; and if he had been less hasty in expression, less summary in thought, I doubt whether he need have appealed to it at all. But my task is to analyse his philosophical principles, not to decide whether he always made the best possible use of them; and this very hastiness of expression is instructive so far as it throws into relief the principle by which he attempted, however unsuccessfully, to justify it.

6 *THE ANTI-HISTORICISM OF RUSKIN'S CONTEMPORARIES*

These observations must suffice for the present as an outline of Ruskin's philosophy. The important point about the various principles which I have enumerated is their close interconnexion; they form a philosophical "ring" of exceedingly solid texture, capable of supporting great strains without damage. I have said that hastiness of expression was a besetting sin of Ruskin's; but it was a defect only rendered possible by the solidity and compactness of his philosophy, which enabled him to think and act quickly where a man with a less homogeneous mind would have stumbled and groped.

But this whole-hearted historicism only accentuated his opposition to the philosophers of his day. Of the older or Scottish school we need not speak; its influence was already waning, though we have seen how it left its mark on *Modern Painters*. But there was also a younger school, which on a basis of Scottish psychology had constructed a new system out of the less profound things in Kant. This was represented on different sides by Sir William Hamilton, whose work began to attract attention about 1830, and Coleridge, who from 1800 to 1834 was engaged in popularising some of the features of Kant's system in a brilliant and original manner.

Now the fundamental assumptions of the Kantian system—at least as interpreted by these disciples—were the very opposite of everything that Ruskin instinctively believed. In the first place, Kantianism was utterly unhistorical. Kant, with his vast equipment of scientific knowledge, was by comparison uninterested in history, and had no real sympathy with any historical period outside his own times. The germs of Hegelian historicism are present in Kant, but they can easily be overlooked; and it is not surprising to find that his philosophy could be interpreted as a thoroughgoing example of the logical view of contradiction, namely that of two contrary propositions one must be false; and any member of the school would have looked upon Ruskin's language about polygonal matters of fact as a sophistical joke in rather bad taste. Again, the Kantians firmly believed in the reality of distinctions within the mind. It was a habit learned from the Scottish psychologists, and justified, they thought, by their studies in Kant.

Ruskin, as I have remarked, thought of art, religion, and politics as alternative manifestations of the same indivisible spirit, acting and reacting on each other with perfect freedom. The Kantians on the contrary believed that the mind had a number of different faculties which worked, to all intents and purposes, in so many watertight

compartments. They began by making a distinction between the theoretical and practical functions, knowing
and acting: and then went on to distinguish, on the
theoretical side, reason and understanding. It was in
criticism of the philosophical abuses to which these distinctions opened the door that Carlyle uttered his well-
known gibe about Coleridge, that he had learnt the trick
of believing with his reason what his understanding knew
to be impossible. Carlyle—and Ruskin fully agreed with
him—thought that nothing but harm could come of
this distinction-drawing[13] which had been the chief oc-
cupation of English philosophy ever since, after Hume,
it lost its nerve for speculation.

This Kantian movement in the first half of the nineteenth century had at least one result of the very highest
importance. Kant himself had seemed to suggest that the
theoretical faculty of the mind—the knowing faculty—
was incapable of arriving at ultimate truth, and that in
the supreme issues of philosophy and religion the practical or moral faculty was the only guide. This idea sank
very deeply into the minds of the English Kantians, and
by them it was so effectually popularised as to dominate
the entire thought of the Victorian age. The agnosticism
which was on the whole the most popular variety of "advanced thought" throughout that period may be traced
back in a direct line from Huxley through Herbert
Spencer, Dean Mansel, and Hamilton, to Kant. During
the whole of the central and later Victorian period it was
usual for educated and thoughtful Englishmen to believe
as a matter of course that the mind has two faculties, the
theoretical and the practical, and that the theoretical was
fundamentally unreliable, while the practical was always trustworthy. Thus, they held, you could never settle
questions of ultimate, absolute truth, and it was no good

13. "Modern philosophy is a great separator." *Ethics of the Dust*, 108.

trying: but moral questions you could and must settle. So it became the fashion to despair of solving difficult intellectual problems, while moral problems of at least equal difficulty were held to be soluble without hesitation, by the employment of the faculty called conscience, which you had only to obey and all would be well.

This combination of intellectual scepticism with moral dogmatism[14] is so characteristic of the Victorian age that I think you will find it to be the leading feature of the philosophy of that period, taken as a whole. Its effect on the general temper of the age was nothing short of disastrous. It inculcated moral narrowness combined with intellectual apathy, and made the Victorian Englishman appear in the eyes of the world as a prig and a Philistine, religious in it, proud of his ignorance, confident in his monopoly of a sense of justice and "fair play," and boasting of an educational system which did not stuff a boy's head with facts, still less with ideas, but taught him to behave like a gentleman. It was the same fallacy that underlay the typically Victorian suggestion that the doctrines of Christian belief should be given up as being incapable of proof, while the Christian ethics should be preserved, as the best ethical system in existence.

From this specifically Victorian heresy, this intellectual disease which ate like a canker into the whole life of the nineteenth century, Ruskin was entirely and astonishingly free. Most of his contemporaries were tainted with it. Browning himself,[15] to mention one only, in the last

14. The rise of Pragmatism at the end of the Victorian era represents a revival of the "Victorian Heresy" in protest against the idealism of Hegelian origin—as Victorianism and Pragmatism are Kantian—which threatened to destroy it.

15. This has been shown with admirable clearness by Sir Henry Jones in his book on *Browning as a Philosophical and Religious Teacher*. Dean Inge is mistaken (*Outspoken Essays*, p. 192) in suggesting that the tendency overcame Browning late in life when his powers were perhaps failing; for it nowhere appears more strikingly than in the plot of *Paracelsus*.

resort despaired of the intellect with which he was so generously endowed, and fell back almost with relief on a blind and irrational faith. But there is not the smallest trace of it in the whole works of Ruskin. If he was ever tempted to suggest that the human intellect was by its inherent limitations debarred from solving certain problems—and he does so speak, in later life, of theological difficulties—he at least never gives back with one hand what he has taken away with the other, or supposes that "conscience" or "faith" may guide us where "intellect" breaks down.

The current of philosophical thought in England was thus absolutely alien to Ruskin's mind. It was not till the seventies, when a few enterprising young men in Oxford began to expound Hegel to their pupils, that ideas akin to those which formed Ruskin's philosophy became part of the main stream of academic thought in this country. Ruskin had been applying in practice since 1840 the philosophical system of which the theory was first published in English in 1865 by James Hutchison Stirling in that queer, incoherent, isolated book "The Secret of Hegel," and was taken up in the following decade by Wallace and Bradley and others, and in a modified form by T. H. Green, at Oxford.

This, surely, explains Ruskin's attitude to the philosophers of his own day. They were occupied exclusively with the logic of the eighteenth century; abstract, formalistic, unhistorical; largely concerned with imaginary anatomies of the human mind. He was proceeding on the basis of a totally different philosophy, the nineteenth-century historical idealism; supple where the other was rigid, sympathetic where it was hostile; interested in facts where the other cared only for generalities; seizing the character of individual minds as a whole where the other saw only disjointed psychological states; a rich soil for poetry and art while the other starved and stunted the imagination. Little wonder that Ruskin was no friend to philosophers, when he compared their philosophies with the philosophy of his own inmost consciousness.

But it was not only the academic philosophers who were affected by the logicism and Kantianism against which Ruskin rebelled. The old logic and psychology, which the new Kantianism had done little to modify, were deeply rooted in the English popular consciousness, and affected every kind of activity and every branch of thought. Ruskin's intellectual loneliness has often been noticed, but its cause has never been fully understood. He was at cross-purposes with his age: all the fundamental assumptions which underlay his thought contradicted those which underlay that of his contemporaries. Unless he is an egotist, a man is not unhappy when people disagree with his expressed opinions. He merely falls to arguing with them. But you cannot argue with people who dissent from your unexpressed convictions. You have no common ground on which to argue. The only cure is to turn philosopher and drag your convictions and theirs into the daylight. Ruskin was not an egotist: he was lonely and dissatisfied not because people rejected his opinions but because they rejected his philosophy. In face of this attitude he was powerless; for, being no philosopher, he could not analyse the real nature of the conflict between himself and his age, and so could not get the conflict fought out to an issue. It was always a fight in the dark.

If it was his philosophy that deprived him of other intellectual companionship, it was his philosophy that gave him the one friendship which can truly be called by that name. Carlyle was a student of German philosophy, but Ruskin specially exempts him from the curse which he lays upon philosophers generally. Why was this? It is a curious fact that Carlyle was not, like Coleridge,[16] a Kantian. He was a follower of Fichte, and with Fichte the process had already begun which transmutes Kant into Hegel. In some ways Fichte is nearer to Ruskin than to the Kantians whom they both detested.

7 *THE UNITY OF THE SPIRIT:*
COROLLARIES AND ILLUSTRATIONS

I promised to give you a few illustrations of the way in which Ruskin's historical tendencies, and especially his belief in the unity of the mind, influenced his practical thinking. I am the more anxious to do this, because nothing in all Ruskin's work is more striking than the way in which he uses this conviction as a philosophical weapon.

It is a conviction which necessarily issues in a synthetic habit of mind—a habit, I mean, of laying stress on the resemblances and connexions between problems, instead of regarding every problem as intrinsically different from every other. And it is natural that this, again, should result in a frequent appeal to the argument by analogy. Especially is this the case when the analogy is between various activities or functions of the mind. If you believe that these various activities proceed from different "faculties," then clearly you do not hold yourself justified in

16. There were elements of Schelling in Coleridge. But the abstractness of Schellingism (the "night in which all cows are black") deprives it of just the character of historical concreteness that Ruskin wanted; and Coleridge even exaggerates Schelling's abstractness.

transferring to one of these faculties a statement which
has been proved to hold good of another. But if you believe that there is no such thing as the distinction between
faculties, then whatever holds good of one human activity
necessarily holds good of all. Strictly speaking therefore
this argument is not analogical: for the relation between
two instances of a universal law is not one of analogy.

Thus, in the third volume of *Modern Painters* Ruskin
answers certain critics who had accused him of dogmatism
because he had ventured to lay down in a positive and
confident manner principles of right and wrong with
regard to painting. Here is the passage:[17]—

"There are laws of truth and right in painting, just
as fixed as those of harmony in music or of affinity in
chemistry. Those laws are perfectly ascertainable by
labour, and ascertainable no otherwise. It is as ridiculous
for any one to speak positively about painting who has
not given a great part of his life to its study, as it would be
for a person who had never studied chemistry to give a
lecture on affinities of elements; but it is also as ridiculous
for a person to speak hesitatingly about laws of painting
who has conscientiously given time to their ascertain-
ment, as it would be for Mr. Faraday to announce in a
dubious manner that iron had an affinity of oxygen, and
to put it to the vote of his audience whether it had or
not."

You observe here the confidence with which he appeals
to the philosophy of chemistry in order to settle a dis-
puted point in the philosophy of art. He assumes that
chemistry and painting, being each alike an example of
the free activity of the human spirit, are governed by the
same principles and possess the same kind of validity. A
person with less confidence in the unity of the spirit

17. *Modern Painters*, preface to vol. III.; *Works*, 5, 5.

would have declined to assume an analogy between chemistry and painting; and might have gone on to argue that whereas science discovers laws whose truth is the same for everyone, art only reveals beauty, which is a matter of personal taste and knows no law. Ruskin simply sweeps aside all such arguments, unheard, by an appeal to his immutable conviction of the unity of the spirit. What is true of chemistry must on this principle be true of art, and any attempt to prove the contrary is condemned in advance as sophistical.

This analogical method of reasoning is no doubt a dangerous weapon to use; it often misleads, and in unskilled hands may fatally injure the user. But in skilled hands it is a weapon of immense power, clearing the ground of unnecessary argument and accomplishing a vast amount of varied work with the least possible waste of energy; while the alternative method, with all its virtues, is always immensely slow in action and immensely wasteful of power.

Secondly, his conviction of the unity of the mind provides, I believe, the explanation of perhaps the greatest difficulty in all Ruskin's works—his doctrine as to the relation between art and nature. His insistence upon the accurate literal portrayal of nature as the essence of good art—his frequent assertion that the only value a work of art possesses is that it should be an accurate record of a worthy subject—his lack of interest in works of art which did not represent a subject that pleased him—these facts are, from the point of view of most modern artists and critics, grave defects in his art-criticism, Taken literally, as Ruskin himself generally took them, they are at any rate questionable; and they caused him not a little trouble when he came, for instance to defend the topographical licence of Turner, or to expound the function of imagination in art. But it seems to me that all this side of his art-criticism—the anti-imaginative, anti-artistic side, if you like—is a sympton of his belief in the unity and solidarity of the human spirit. He is out to deny that art is a thing by itself, which can thrive in a vacuum, cut off from the general interests of humanity. The soil in which art grows is not art but life. Art is expression, and it cannot arise until men have something to express. When you feel so strongly about something—the joys or sorrows of your domestic or national life: the things you see round you: your religious beliefs, and so on—that you must at all costs express your feelings, then art is born. And so you cannot encourage art by teaching people the manual knack of drawing, and hoping that the feeling will come of itself. If you could only teach people to feel, they would teach themselves to draw, fast enough. The problem is not, in Ruskin's own words, how to give gentlemen an artist's education; it is how to give artists a gentleman's education.

The cry of Art for Art's sake, issuing as it did from the analytic or separative tendency in the Victorian mind, expresses everything against which Ruskin was here in revolt. It assumed that Art—with a capital A—was the product of a quite special and unique faculty, and that this faculty had nothing to gain and everything to lose by being worried with irrelevant issues like morality and religion and everyday life. Art could only flourish in properly heated and hermetically sealed rooms, whose heavy curtains kept out every trace of sunshine and all the noises of the world's business. Such a conception of art as this was, I believe, the enemy at which Ruskin was tilting when he laid stress on the importance of the subject in art. He was trying to express the idea that art, to be healthy, must strike its roots deep into the common earth of life, with all its interests and passions and prejudices. He may have mis-stated and at times even misunderstood this idea; but I am convinced that this was the idea which his doctrine of the relation between art and nature aimed at expressing.

Thirdly: the same synthetic view of the human mind has important results in his treatment of history. He notices, and often recurs to it as a mysterious fact, that the attainment of perfection in art seems to herald the downfall of a civilisation, while a high state of moral nobility may coexist with a complete absence of art. Now why is this fact, if it is a fact, so striking to Ruskin? Only because of his profound belief in the unity of the spirit. Without that belief, he would have replied, when the question was raised, "Why shouldn't a man be a good artist and a bad man? Why shouldn't a virtuous man be artistically incompetent? What reason on earth is there to suppose that excellence in morals and in art need ever go together, and why should we be surprised if they don't."

But Ruskin believed that morality issues, not from a moral faculty, but from the nature of the whole man, and so with art; and if the self which you reveal in morality is bad, how can the same self, when you reveal it in terms of art, be good?

His successive attempts to solve this problem are curious. In the *Two Paths*, where it is seriously raised for the first time, he tries to dispose of it by the theory that conventional art depraves, while naturalistic art exalts; or rather, if we may correct this phraseology by reference to other passages[18] which express his meaning more care-

18. I refer especially to *The Cestus of Aglaia: Works*, 19, 57: "Good pictures do not teach a nation: they are a sign of its having been taught." And to such passages as *Modern Painters*, part IV., ch. ix., § 1, where beauty is compared to the blossom growing on the stem of truth. Art is almost always regarded by Ruskin as proceeding "out

fully, conventional art is symptomatic of moral depravity
and naturalistic art of moral integrity. The first lecture
in *The Two Paths* is a striking exposition of this view,
which we may interpret by saying that the art of a healthy
nation is a direct expression of its spontaneous interest
in life, while the art of an enfeebled and corrupt nation
forgets its relation to reality and loses itself in technicali-
ties and aestheticisms, in abstract canons and formal restrictions.

This may all be true enough, but every reader must
see that is beside the point. The problem stated at the
beginning of the lecture is never really faced at all. You
remember how it is stated.[19]

"The period in which any given people reach their
highest power in art is precisely that in which they appear
to sign the warrant of their own ruin; [and that], from
the moment in which a perfect statue appears in Florence,
a perfect picture in Venice, or a perfect fresco in Rome,
from that hour forward, probity, industry, and courage
seem to be exiled from their walls, and they perish in a
sculpturesque paralysis, or a many-coloured corruption."

Now this problem is not solved. This distinction be-

---

of the abundance of the heart"—a spontaneous overflow of the life
of a man or a nation, truly reflecting his nature but not, necessarily,
reacting on it. But there are several occasions about 1858 on which
Ruskin seems to ascribe a direct influence to art.

19. *Two Paths*, Lecture I., 5. *Cf.* Lecture III., 93: "The names of
the great painters are like passing bells." (It is a curious and significant
fact that Hegel in a famous passage makes exactly the same remark
about the highest developments of philosophy.) I have omitted
certain other passages in which Ruskin deals with the same problem.
The most interesting is in *Works* 16, 196 (*Cambridge Inaugural*, 1858:
between the first and second lectures of *The Two Paths* in date). Here
the suggested solution depends on distinguishing between art followed
only for the sake of luxury or delight, and art used to teach truth or
supposed truth. I presume that Ruskin did not reprint this lecture
in *The Two Paths* because he meant the Bradford lecture to stand as
a better restatement of the same line of thought.

tween naturalistic and conventional art does not touch it. It simply evades it. Michael Angelo and Tintoret were not blind conventionalists. They exemplified all the virtues of truth, earnestness and sincerity which Ruskin here ascribes to naturalistic art and to that alone. And yet it was their work that heralded the downfall of Florence and Venice.

Conscious of his failure, he returns to the same problem in the Bradford lecture (*Two Paths*, Lecture III.). Here a new solution is offered. The great art-periods of the past were fatal to national life because art has always been in the service of a rich and proud nobility, careless of the misery in which its less fortunate neighbours lay. This solution, in itself a fertile suggestion, again fails, hardly less flagrantly. For if the art of Tintoret served to glorify a brutal, proud, and callous Venetian nobility, and to express their ideals, it must itself be brutal, proud, and callous: which Ruskin does not admit. Indeed, he notices chiefly in Tintoret (*Two Paths*, Appendix) his kindness, humility, and intense sensibility.

Later, in the Oxford Lectures, he returned to the problem yet again, and qualified it through a new and better understanding of its elements. In *The Two Paths* he had expressed his wonder that any race gifted with such sublime moral qualities as the Scottish Highlanders should be utterly destitute of art. It is a curious judgment, and illustrates the danger of leaning too exclusively on one branch of the tree of art. Another traveller in the Highlands did not find the inhabitants so devoid of self-expression.

> Will no one tell me what she sings?
>   Perhaps the plaintive numbers flow
> For old, unhappy, far-off things
>   And battles long ago . . .

It is a strange and mournful thing that the great tradition of music which penetrates every recess of the Highlands—those songs and pipe-tunes which rise from every shore and every glen, quite literally

> Breaking the silence of the seas
> Among the farthest Hebrides,

should simply have escaped Ruskin's notice.

In the Oxford Lectures he corrects, in part, his mistake. The simple countryman, the artless rustic, is not really such a miracle of moral qualities. The country is not Arcadia; even in the Highlands, humanity is prone to err. And on the other hand, he points out, the countryman is not altogether artless. He has his own simple arts of costume, song, and domestic architecture. Just as travellers report no tribe, however savage, that has not some worship and some idea of deity, so there is no community which does not practise some form of artistic self-expression.

And this goes some way towards solving Ruskin's problem. But it does not solve it entirely; and he never suggests a complete solution. It remains for him a dark and terrible mystery that perfection and death should thus walk hand in hand.

8 RUSKIN AND BROWNING

And yet is it so very mysterious? The perfection of any one artistic style or social ideal, its complete mastery, at once lays a dilemma before the human spirit: either go on repeating the perfection that has been attained, become merely imitative, or else launch out into the void, feeling for a new style or a new ideal, and acquiescing in the death of the old. Such a death is in every way preferable to the decrepitude which is its only alternative. "What's come to perfection perishes," says Browning, in handling the same problem;[20] the perfect mastery of Titian and Tintoret demonstrates that Venice has achieved what she was aiming at, and in that direction can achieve no more. After that nothing remains but to return, earth to earth, dust to dust, in hope of a resurrection. "Venice spent what Venice earned."

Here, as often, Browning had the clearer vision. If one compares the minds of the two men, one seems to see that Browning is always more successful in detail. He never goes wildly wrong as Ruskin so often does. He has more sense than to say, for instance, that[21] because trees have pointed leaves therefore the pointed form must be one most fitted for perpetual contemplation by the human mind, and therefore all windows ought to have pointed tops. Browning had not Ruskin's dashing recklessness; until he had carefully thought round his subject, he did not speak at all. So the works of Browning studied in detail give a much better impression than those of Ruskin, which are painful to read in full on account of their chaotic haste and effusiveness—their author's habit of immediate and impetuous speech on any and every

20. *Old Pictures in Florence*: a poem whose purpose is to justify Browning's taste for the primitive Italian painters in face of their obvious inferiority in scope, power, and technique to their successors. The argument of the poem turns on the fact that the later and more perfect art carries in it the seeds of decay, which spoil the pleasure of the spectator with their presentiment of doom: while the work of the primitives seems exempt from all taint of mortality. Ruskin admitted (*Modern Painters*, part v., ch. xx : *Works*, 6, 449) that *The Bishop Orders his Tomb* anticipated his own views, expressed in *The Stones of Venice*, on the Italian Renaissance: he did not apparently observe the connexion between *Old Pictures* and the present problem.

21. Edinburgh *Lectures on Architecture*: *Works*, 12, 30.

subject. But come down to fundamentals, and you see at once that Ruskin's was the greater mind of the two. Browning was by comparison unsound on ultimate issues. This is indicated (to go no further) by two facts: his agnosticism and his optimism. I have already referred to his agnosticism, and pointed out how this implies a taint of the current Victorian Kantianism, from which Ruskin was saved by the soundness of his philosophical instincts. Browning's optimism is a parallel case.

It is sometimes imagined that anyone who has a philosophy at all must be either an optimist or a pessimist, and that one of a philosopher's duties is to argue out the issue between these two creeds and decide which to adopt. As a matter of fact optimism and pessimism are not philosophies at all: they are diseases. The reason why one man is an optimist and another a pessimist is not to be sought in philosophical argument; it is to be sought in mental pathology. No philosopher worthy of the name has ever been in the ordinary sense of the word[22] either an optimist or a pessimist; and Ruskin was neither, simply because his philosophical instinct was too sound to let him fall into such snares. Browning, less sound on fundamentals, slid into optimism, and in so doing went far to destroy the value of his contribution to Victorian thought.

22. In this (debased) sense optimism means the belief that, ultimately, things are all right, and pessimism the belief that, ultimately, they are all wrong. Thus during the war a pessimist meant a person who believed the Germans were going to win. The term optimism has also a proper or philosophical sense, viz: the doctrine that this world is "the best of all possible worlds," i.e. that a better world, though perhaps imaginable, could not really exist, a doctrine connected with the great name of Leibnitz. It is only by a gross confusion of thought such as is revealed by Voltaire's *Candide* that this doctrine (that evils are necessary and inseparable from the very existence of a world) can be mistaken for optimism in the ordinary sense. But Leibnitz' theory is now only of historical interest.

9 *CONCLUSION*

Bearing all this in mind, I think it is not too much to say that Ruskin was in philosophy the best-equipped mind of his generation. The philosophical weapons with which he was provided could smash their way through Coleridge's vague distinctions or Mill's pettifogging logic as easily as Hegel's dialectic could batter Kant or Hume out of recognition at ten miles' range. He did not always handle his guns as well as they deserved, and he sometimes fell back on a secondary armament of obsolete weapons: but when he did get the sights on and began making good practice he annihilated.

The overwhelming superiority of Ruskin's intellectual armament consisted in this fact: that, in an age which was turning from the ideal of abstract, logical, doctrinaire thinking to an ideal of concrete, historical, imaginative thinking, Ruskin alone of Englishmen refrained from putting his new wine into the old bottles of eighteenth-century philosophy. Coleridge, Mill and the rest tried to combine nineteenth-century practice with eighteenth-century principles; and their out-of-date philosophy hampered them at every turn. Ruskin, more independent and original than they, flung his whole mind into the new movement of thought: and that is why, when everyone else was moving stiffly, their feet clogged with the mud of ancient theories, Ruskin alone seems perfectly at his ease, never worried by the care of making ends meet, flying through the air of thought with the freedom and security of a Tintoret angel.

I say he was philosophically the best-equipped mind of his generation. Book-learned in philosophy he was not;

but he was no great believer in book-learning. He once laughed at "foolish readers" who doubted the truth of his economic views because he said he had never read books on political economy. "Did they suppose," he asks,[23] "I had got my knowledge of art by reading books?" His philosophical ideas cannot be directly traced to the influence of authors whom he had read, any more than his views on painting or economics. And so I am not concerned to ask what were the sources of his philosophy. It is the character of that philosophy that I wish to make clear to you: its historical and dialectical, as opposed to a mathematical and logical, character; its scorn of scholastic distinctions; its breadth and imaginativeness; above all, its intensely synthetic nature—its refusal to separate any one aspect of life from any other, and its resolute envisagement of the spirit as a single and indivisible whole. Mazzini expressed his opinion of Ruskin's intellect by describing it as the most analytic mind in Europe. This may have been true; but it was the least important part of the truth. Ruskin's greatness lay not in his analytic but in his synthetic power. There were then, and always are, plenty of analytic minds. It is the synthetic mind— the mind that sees the unity of things—that is rare; and it is to this class that Ruskin pre-eminently belongs.

23. *Two Paths*, § 189, footnote (added in later editions): *Works*, 16, 406.

Outlines of a Philosophy of Art

AUTHOR'S PREFACE

August 1924

THIS BOOK aims at doing two things: stating a general conception of art, and developing its consequences. The general conception here maintained is not new; it is one already familiar from the works of Coleridge, Croce, and many others; it is the view that art is at bottom neither more nor less than imagination. But when one has arrived at such a conception, the question is what to do next. One may advertise its merits by applying it to numerous examples and showing how neatly it fits them; but this soon degenerates into a conjuring trick which the audience has seen through. Or one may criticize other people's views; but this is apt to be a mere washing of dirty linen in public. Or one may frankly begin talking about something else, and fill up the book with observations on art and artists. There remains a more difficult course: to develop the conception itself in such a way as to lay bare the implications contained in it. This is perhaps the only course that deserves the name of philos-

Outlines of a Philosophy of Art. London: Oxford University Press, 1925.

45

ophy. For philosophy lives in its own details; and it ought to treat each detail as a fresh problem, with a place of its own in the general body of philosophical thought, and not as another lock to be opened with the same skeleton key, or as one which for that very reason is not worth opening.

There are certain subordinate conceptions contained within the general conception of art: the sublime, the comic, and the forms of beauty in general; the antitheses of nature and art, formal art and naturalistic art, classical and romantic art, genius and taste, matter and form; notions like that of technique; distinctions between the various so-called arts; and the like. To reduce these to so many cases of art, and to leave it at that, is to fall a victim to the skeleton-key habit, to convert the philosophy of art into a night in which all cows are black. These conceptions have their own value in their own place, and it ought to be possible not only to admit this fact in the abstract but to demonstrate it by showing what their place is: which means showing them to be involved in the conception of art as such, to be distinctions into which that conception articulates itself.

The greater part of the following essay is an attempt to carry out this programme. The general conception of art and of its place in life, here stated in the first and last chapters, has been formulated in the writer's book called *Speculum Mentis*; but the other chapters are concerned with these detailed articulations, which the plan of the earlier work perforce excluded.

The result is no more than an outline. Comparatively few of the possible topics have been discussed, and those as briefly as possible, with little in the way of illustration or explanation; while criticism and reference to the history of the subject have been altogether excluded. But the attempt to cover much ground in few words is an attempt always worth making; and if the result is found worth reading, the reader as well as the writer must thank the Delegates of the Clarendon Press, without whose invitation the book would not have been written.

1   THE GENERAL NATURE OF ART

§ 1   The Problem

The word art has in ordinary usage three senses. First, it means the creation of objects or the pursuit of activities called works of art, by people called artists; these works being distinguished from other objects and acts not merely as human products, but as products intended to be beautiful. Secondly, it means the creation of objects or the pursuit of activities called artificial as opposed to natural; that is to say objects created or activities pursued by human beings consciously free to control their natural impulses and to organize their life on a plan. Thirdly, it means that frame of mind which we call artistic, the frame of mind in which we are aware of beauty.

This is not a mere linguistic accident or an ambiguity in the word art. There is a real relation between the three things enumerated above, which is revealed by the fact that the first is the sum of the second and third. Art, in the sense in which we call sculpture or music an art, differs from art in the sense in which agriculture or navigation is an art in one point only: namely in being controlled or dominated by art in the sense of the awareness of beauty.

Since the controlling element in the so-called "arts" of

sculpture, music and the rest is the awareness of beauty, the central notion in the philosophy of art is the notion of a specific activity by which we apprehend objects as beautiful. Fundamentally, fine art is this apprehension of beauty. Where this is present, it will find out a way to create objects which shall express itself; where it is absent, no degree of technical skill in the creation of objects will take its place or conjure it into existence. The awareness of beauty is at once the starting-point and the culmination, the presupposition and the end, of all art. His awareness of beauty is the initial impulse in obedience to which a painter begins to paint a picture; it is by this same awareness that he decides, at every moment of the process, what to do to his picture next; and it is simply an enlargement and a sharpening of the same awareness that constitute, either for him or for anyone else, the value of the picture when it is done.

The philosophy of art is the attempt to discover what art is; and this involves not an examination of the world around us in order to discover and analyse instances of it, as if it were a chemical substance, but a reflection upon our own activities, among which art has its place. But if there are three different activities that go by the name of art, which of these do we propose to investigate? The answer is, that if the three senses of the word art are connected by a real and necessary bond, the philosophy of art cannot confine itself to any one of them, to the exclusion of the others. It must begin by studying that which is most fundamental, the awareness of beauty; it must go on to study the distinction between the natural and the artificial, and to show how this distinction arises; and it must end by studying that special form of production in which the artificial object is a work of art. And it must justify this programme by showing that its three parts are connected in such a way that they cannot be understood separately.

But art is only one of a number of activities; and to answer the question what art is can only mean placing it in its relation to our other activities. Hence the only possible philosophy of art is a general philosophy of man and his world with special reference to man's function as an artist and his world's aspect of beauty.

In this case, as in all other cases, the form and order of the exposition must in a sense invert the form and order of inquiry. In trying to arrive at an understanding of any activity, one must begin with a mass of experience relative to that activity; and this experience cannot be acquired by philosophical thinking, or by scientific experiments, or by observation of the activity in other people, but only by a long and specialized pursuit of the activity itself. Only after this experience has been acquired is it possible to reflect upon it and bring to light the principles underlying it. To expound the philosophy of an activity is to expound these principles in their general character and their implications; and such an exposition may deceive unwary readers into thinking that the writer is trying to deduce the features of a certain field of activity altogether *a priori* and in abstraction from actual experience, when he is really trying to communicate his reflections upon his own experience to readers who have been through the same experience themselves.

§ 2 *Art in its Generic Nature*

For the present, then, art is to mean the special activity by which we apprehend beauty. This implies that there are various activities of which we have experience, and that art has certain features in common with them all and others peculiar to itself; to determine its general nature therefore involves distinguishing its generic nature on the one hand and its specific nature on the other. Definition, according to the principles of formal logic, must proceed by genus and differentia.

It is important to make this distinction at the outset, because reflection upon activities like art or religion very often frustrates itself by confusing a generic with a specific feature. Every activity is in certain ways very much like any other; and people who are trying to describe their own experience of art, religion, science and so forth constantly select for emphasis features due not to the special character of the activity but to the fact that they have had special experience of it. For instance, religion is described as giving knowledge of ultimate reality, which is precisely what artists claim for art, scientists for science, and philosophers for philosophy; or as giving a sense of victory over one's lower nature, of peace, of security, which are feelings involved in any activity whatever, provided it is pursued earnestly and successfully; and so forth. The same error, upon a larger scale, appears in the attempt to equate various activities with the three aspects of the mental life which are distinguished by analytic psychology: cognition, conation and emotion. This threefold distinction has a very real value, but it becomes a fantastic mythology if it is mistaken for a distinction between three activities which can exist separately, or of which one can predominate over the other, or of which one can undergo a modification without producing corresponding modifications in the other.

In every field of activity there is a theoretical element, in virtue of which the mind is aware of something; there is a practical element in virtue of which the mind is bringing about a change in itself and in its world; and there is

an element of feeling, in virtue of which the mind's cog-
nitions and actions are coloured with desire and aversion,
pleasure and pain. In no case is any one of these elements
active without the others; they are correlative elements
in every act and every experience, and make up a single
indivisible whole. But the theoretical element is not always knowledge in the strict sense of the word; knowledge
is the highest form of theoretical activity, not equivalent
to that activity in general: and in the same way moral
action, though the highest form of practical activity, is
not found wherever practical activity is found. And each
specific form of theory, practice or feeling involves corresponding forms of the other two elements, and cannot
exist in the absence of these.

Merely in virtue of its generic character as an activity,
therefore, art is at once theoretical, practical and emotional. It is theoretical: that is, in art the mind has an object which it contemplates. But this object is an object
of a specific kind, peculiar to itself; it is not God, or
natural law, or historical fact, or philosophical truth; and
because it is specifically different from the object of religion or science or history or philosophy, the act of
contemplating it must also be a specifically peculiar kind
of act. Art is practical: that is, in art the mind is trying to
realize an ideal, to bring itself into a certain state and at
the same time to bring its world into a certain state. But
this ideal is not expediency or duty, and the mind's activity in art is therefore not a utilitarian or a moral activity. And again, art is emotional: that is, it is a life of
pleasure and pain, desire and aversion, intertwined, as
these opposite feelings always are, in such a way that each
is conditioned by the felt or implied presence of the
other. But these feelings are in the case of art tinged with
a colour of their own; the artist's pleasure is not the pleas-

ure of the voluptuary or the scientist or the man of action, but a specifically aesthetic pleasure.

Art, religion, science, and so forth, which are here treated as species of a genus called activity, are in reality related to one another in a way which is not exactly that of co-ordinate species. This point will be taken up again and dealt with more fully in the last chapter. For the present it is sufficient to point out that the logic of genus and species is at this stage of the inquiry used as the first approximation to a truth which it does not exhaust.

§ 3 *Art in its Specific Nature:*
     Theoretically, as Imagination

In art there are always a subject and an object, a contemplator and something contemplated. But the subject's activity, the object's nature, and the character of the relation between them have certain peculiarities which distinguish the case of art from other cases. What the subject does is to imagine: the object is an imaginary object, and the relation between them is that the individual or empirical act of imagining creates the object. In knowledge, on the other hand, the object is real; and the relation between them is that the empirical act of knowing presupposes the object and does not create it. This may be said without prejudice to the idealistic view that there is an absolute or transcendental sense in which knowing creates its object; for no idealist is so innocent as to confuse knowledge with imagination and to suppose that what we generally call knowing is simply imagining.

The object, in the case of art, is an imaginary object, not a real object. Shakespeare's printed text is a real object, and really lies before me; but to contemplate the tragedy of *Hamlet* is not to perceive this printed book but to "see" Hamlet himself as Shakespeare "saw" him. This "seeing" is the contemplation of a human character, human words, human actions; but the character, words, and actions of an imaginary human being. No doubt the story of Hamlet is derived from that of Olaf Cuaran; but Hamlet himself is not Olaf Cuaran but an imaginary person ultimately suggested by Olaf Cuaran. Consequently our own attitude towards Hamlet is that we do not know him, we imagine him. If we say that we know Hamlet to have killed his uncle, what we mean is either that we imagine him doing so, which is true, or that we know that Shakespeare imagined him doing so, which is also true, or that Hamlet was a real person who really did kill his uncle, which is untrue. Further, the Hamlet that we imagine is created by our act of imagining him; the Hamlet that Shakespeare imagined, by Shakespeare's act of imagining him; and these two Hamlets, though they may resemble each other, are not identical. Whereas the London that I know and the London that you know are the same London, and this London does not depend for its existence on your personal acquaintance with it, nor yet on mine.

But *Hamlet* would be neither more nor less of a great tragedy if, as might conceivably have happened, Olaf Cuaran had been just the kind of man, and had said and done just the things, that Shakespeare imagined Hamlet being and saying and doing. In that case the object would be real, and our imagining would apparently give place to knowing. But if art is imagining, does it not follow that the result would not be art?

It would follow, if the imaginary and the real excluded one another; and we certainly do use the word imaginary with a definite implication of unreality. But if I imagine Kubla Khan's palace in "Xanadu," this act is none the

less an act of imagination because Shantu is a real town in
China; nor would it be any the less an act of imagination
if it happened that the real Kubla Khan had really built
such a palace there. To imagine an object is not to commit oneself in thought to its unreality; it is to be wholly
indifferent to its reality. An imaginary object, therefore,
is not an unreal object but an object about which we do
not trouble to ask whether it is real or unreal. The imaginary is not the opposite of the real, but the indifferent
identity of the real and its opposite. Thus Shakespeare
embodies history and fiction side by side in certain of his
plays, but the plays are not mixtures of history and art,
truth and beauty: they are art through and through, because the history and the fiction meet on equal terms; for
the purposes of the play the distinction between them is
non-existent.

And yet we are quite right to oppose the imaginary to
the real. For the real is only real as it stands in the real
world; and a fragment of history embedded in a work of
fiction, by losing its real context and acquiring a fictitious
context, becomes itself tainted with fiction. A lie that is
half a truth becomes a lie throughout, because the false
half infects the true half and twists it into a misrepresenta-
tion of the facts. Hence a work of art which indifferently
includes fact and fiction becomes, by that mere indifference, pure fiction, though no doubt a fiction founded on
fact.

To imagine is to refrain from making a distinction
which we make whenever we think: the distinction between reality and unreality, truth and falsehood. Therefore imagining is not a kind of thinking, nor is thinking
a kind of imagining, for each negates the specific nature
of the other. Yet these two different activities are not
wholly unrelated. Thinking is making a distinction be-

tween truth and falsehood; but this presupposes a phase of consciousness in which this distinction is not made. That which we deny or think false must be first imagined, or there is nothing to deny: that which we assert or think true must first be imagined, or else we could not ask whether it was true without assuming that it was true. Hence the relation between imagination and thought is that thought presupposes imagination, but imagination does not presuppose thought.

§ 4 *The Primitiveness of Art*

This fact is of crucial importance for the attempt to determine the place of art in life as a whole. As thinking presupposes imagining, all those activities whose theoretical aspect takes the form of thought presuppose art; and art is the basis of science, history, "common sense," and so forth. Art is the primary and fundamental activity of the mind, the original soil out of which all other activities grow. It is not a primitive form of religion or science or philosophy, it is something more primitive than these, something that underlies them and makes them possible.

This doctrine of the primitiveness of art runs counter to a certain view which was very widespread in the nineteenth century and still affects a great deal of our ordinary thinking: the view of art as an aristocratic activity, a higher and more specialized type of consciousness than perception of the "common-sense" world or religious or scientific thought. This notion encouraged a certain habit of self-adulation among artists, which went to great lengths in the aestheticism of the later nineteenth century; and it would be difficult to quarrel with such an attitude if the philosophy on which it was founded were true, and if art really were a more highly-developed and logically advanced activity than others; for in that case the artist would certainly be a spiritual aristocrat, related to other people as a mature man to children.

On the other hand, the doctrine of the primitiveness of art is slowly forcing itself upon us as we come to know more of the mental life of children and savages. We find that children who are quite incapable of advanced scientific and philosophical thinking constantly show a high degree of artistic power. Most children can extemporise verses and songs better than their elders; many of them invent excellent stories and draw in a peculiarly forcible and expressive way; and all without exception are at home in a region of imaginative make-believe from which the adult mind feels itself in some degree exiled. The same thing is true of savage and primitive races. The songs and stories, the drawings and carvings and dances of savage peoples are of an excellence quite disproportionate to the same peoples' knowledge and mastery of the world round them. These are familiar facts; but the philosophy which regards art as a highly-specialized activity is in plain conflict with them, and they are only intelligible on the view that art is a relatively primitive function of the mind.

A similar change of view has already taken place with regard to religion. Not many generations ago it was common to consider religion as an "imposture," the fruit of a deliberate policy on the part of rulers, who constituted themselves priests in order to secure their hold over their subjects. That view fell before the recognition, which forced itself on people's minds as they came to know more about uncivilized man, that religion is a more primitive thing than policy, a thing that grows up of itself in the human mind long before that mind reaches the level of deliberate political thought. But we are still so far dominated by the corresponding error about art that we feel surprise at the artistic achievements of children and savages; and modern anthropology seeks for a religious motive in the art of palaeolithic man precisely as eighteenth-century philosophers sought for a political motive in the religious organization of primitive peoples.

To say that art is the primary activity of the mind implies that art arises of itself and does not depend on the previous development of any other activity. It is not a kind of modified perception; nor is it a kind of modified religion. It is on the contrary that of which both perception and religion are modifications. When a child playing on the shore says "the water likes it when I dig a river for it to run in," he is not presupposing or assuming any belief in a water-sprite; he is performing an act of imagination which is the basis upon which all beliefs of this kind are erected. The fantasies of the poetic imagination are the material out of which religion constructs its mythology, not vice versa. Most current speculation about the origin of religion fails through not recognizing that it presupposes poetic imagery; and hence its description of the mental processes involved in animism, magic, and so forth, grotesquely distorts these things into some kind of scientific theory, some analogical or inductive argument, whereas they are at bottom simply imagination. Again, art is not based upon a previous perception of real objects. We do not first ascertain what the object really is and then modify it by allowing our imagination to play upon it. We first imagine; the attempt to ascertain what the object really is involves the attempt to criticize our own imaginations, and hence assumes that we have already imagined.

The aestheticism which regards art as a higher activity than perception or thought seems to be based on two motives. First, it is due to the fact that to an adult and civilized man art is difficult; it costs him a struggle to put himself at the aesthetic or imaginative point of view, and this struggle is taken for a struggle towards a more highly-developed activity, whereas it is in fact a struggle to recapture a more unsophisticated frame of mind. The whole of our education is an education in facing facts; it is designed to lead us away from the world of imagination in which the child lives, and to make us sober and habitual residents in the world of perceptual objects. The child does not struggle to reach the imaginative point of view; he lives habitually in it; but the educated man cannot achieve it except by a struggle, because he must rid himself of the habits imposed upon him by his education, and think himself back into childhood. Secondly, aestheticism confuses the distinction between one kind of art and another with the distinction between art and something else. A view of art which is based exclusively on studying great works of art concludes naturally enough that art is a high and difficult thing, an aristocratic activity, to be approached only by people built on the scale of Dante and Michelangelo; and obviously it takes a greater man to write the *Paradiso* than to see that this is a pen and that twice two is four. But to compare trivial examples of thought—and what we call common sense is only thought at a comparatively trivial level—with great examples of art is not the way to a just comparison. Art includes both the *Paradiso* and a child's scribble or a guttersnipe's discordant whistle; thought includes both the multiplication table and the *Principia*, the perception of a pen and the *Decline and Fall*. If art, in its whole range from highest to lowest, is compared with the whole range of knowledge, the illusion disappears; it becomes clear enough that the artist as such is always a more unsophisticated and primitive spirit than the scientist as such; more of a child in his unstable emotional life, his inability to face facts and to organize his conduct rationally, his comparative crudity of outlook and comparative egotism of temper. Great artists overcome or compensate for these faults in so far as they are great, but continue to show them in so far as they are artists; the weaknesses of the artistic temperament are still visible in a Beethoven or a Dante, however they may be modified and transfigured by his greatness of soul.

Because art is a primitive thing, it does not follow that no one except the child and the savage can be an artist. The grown man remains a child, and the civilized man remains a savage, so far as he preserves any of that fresh and adventurous outlook on life which maturity and civilization may seem to kill; and if, on becoming grown up and civilized, a man really does lose this freshness of heart, and allows himself to be overwhelmed by the shades of the prison-house, then certainly the life of art is for him at an end. But even this is only a temporary eclipse; maturity and civilization have their own art, just because the spiritual life is built on a basis of imagination and can never detach itself from that basis.

On the other hand, the peculiar quality which belongs to the child's art and the savage's art is an imaginative expression of their own childish and savage life, and cannot exist away from that life. To argue from the beauty of Greek vase-painting or medieval sculpture to the conclusion that Greek or medieval life as a whole was beautiful, harmonious, and enlightened, would be as foolish as to suppose that a choir-boy with a beautiful voice must be a model of the virtues, or the author of a Border ballad a respectable citizen. The choir-boy is probably a young rascal, and the author of the Border ballad was probably a brutal and treacherous Border thief; and it is just because of that simplicity and childishness which separates them from the morality of adult civilized men that their art has so tender and innocent a beauty. Educate them, civilize them, and their gift of song will mysteriously vanish. If the Greeks had not been cruel, if the Middle Ages had not been superstitious, the qualities which we find so enchanting would not have been visible in their art. And this is why we cannot emulate Greek vase-paintings and medieval cathedrals, or revive our own folk-songs and country dances. These things were once an integral part of a life which is not only dead but which we would not revive if we could; as no one who remembers his childhood would be a child again for the sake of recapturing the childish keenness of imagination. If we want to paint and build, sing and dance, we must find out how to do it for ourselves.

§ 5 *Art in its Specific Nature:*
   Practically, as the Pursuit of Beauty

Art is imagination; but imagination is an activity. To imagine is not simply to allow a train of images to drift idly across the mind, it is to make an effort to imagine, to work at imagination. One can imagine, as one can do anything else, well or ill; and though one may do it well without taking trouble, one does it on the whole and in the long run better for trying to do it better.

To distinguish an activity as worse or better does not imply referring it to some standard other than itself. If we suspect ourselves of having thought wrongly, there is nothing to do but to think again; thought cannot be checked except by further thought. Similarly, action can only be judged by reference to action. In no case can there be any criterion outside the activity itself, because, if there were, it would be only by this same activity that the criterion was recognized and applied. To imagine well means, therefore, to imagine imaginatively: to live up to a criterion contained in the activity itself. The ideal at which the act of imagining aims is simply the ideal of imagining. But that which art is the attempt to achieve is beauty; and therefore the beautiful is neither more nor less than the imagined.

This implies that it is impossible to imagine anything that is not beautiful; that, in fact, nothing ugly exists, or that, if it does exist, it can never appear to any one. And this seems an outrageous paradox. Nevertheless, it is a truth, and an important truth. Nothing is ugly except in a qualified and relative sense; a picture or a view which is described as ugly is never wholly and simply ugly, but is always a mixture of ugliness and beauty, and it is the presence of the beauty that alone makes the ugliness possible. Nor can such an object be dissected into beautiful parts and ugly parts. It is not that all ugliness is mitigated by streaks of beauty, for this is not necessarily the case; it is rather that all ugliness consists of a beauty, which is actually felt as beautiful, but is in some way frustrated or spoilt. All ugliness is beauty spoilt, beauty uglified. In music, the ugliness of a wrong note depends on the rightness of the other notes; this rightness is musical beauty, and the ugliness of the total effect depends on the destruction of a real and actual beauty by the intrusion of something alien to it, something which yet in itself is not ugly at all, for the wrong note would be right in another key. Ugliness is the destruction of beauty; it presupposes a beauty to be destroyed; and when it has completely destroyed this beauty it ceases to be ugliness and starts fair, so to speak, with a chance of achieving a new beauty of its own. When all sense of key has disappeared because all the notes are wrong notes, one may get the new beauty of keyless sound.

But further, all ugliness, so far as it does actually exist, is not the ugliness of an object imagined but the ugliness of an object not imagined: not imagined, that is, in the strict sense of the word. When a person engaged in thought makes a mistake, we say that he has not really thought; we exhort him to think, and we take it as obvious that one cannot think anything out and at the same time think it falsely. In the same way, when some one imagines something ugly, he has not really imagined; he has not "imagined out" the object, but has been content with half-imagining it. Error is not the absence of thought, nor yet something that is possible when thought is wholly and truly present; it is confused thinking, passing over from thinking this to thinking that without noticing the transition. So ugliness is not the absence of imagination, nor yet something that may happen when imagination in the full sense is present; it is confused imagining, an imagining that slips over from one imagination to another without imagining out any one thing to the end.

Hence comes the idea that ugliness is a low degree of beauty, or that beauty is the perfection which, when missed in varying degrees, gives place to varying degrees of ugliness. But it is clear from what has been said that neither beauty, which is unity, nor ugliness, which is lack of unity, admits of degree. A low degree of beauty means a beauty which we can apprehend with a compara-tively slight exertion of imaginative energy; such a beauty is a trivial, hackneyed, or vulgarized beauty, and these epithets describe it qualitatively.

Beauty is the unity or coherence of the imaginary

object: ugliness its lack of unity, its incoherence. This is no new doctrine; it is generally recognized that beauty is harmony, unity in diversity, symmetry, congruity, or the like. But such phrases are only generic, not specific; for truth also, and utility, and goodness, may all be described in the same kind of language. That which distinguishes beauty from these is that it is not any unity, but an imaginative unity. This is a specific unity whose source is the unity of the act of imagination.

When we imagine, it does not matter what we imagine. There is no external necessity that can circumscribe the possible objects of imagination; each act of imagination creates its object out of nothing and is indifferently free to create anything. But there is an internal necessity which imagination must obey. Whatever we imagine, we must imagine that, and not anything different. We may or may not imagine our hero as dying on the last page; but if we do, we must not imagine anything inconsistent with this. We must "imagine out" his death in all its implications; we must imagine him in a world where a death of this particular kind is possible; we must imagine that his life is such as to expose him to this death. Thus the whole story will be self-coherent; it will be a unity in diversity, a harmony of its various parts. The mere act of imagination, by being itself, by being this act and not a different act, generates in its object that unity which is beauty. But it is clearly possible to imagine different and incompatible things and to waver between one act of imagination and another, to fail to make up one's mind whether one is imagining one version of a story or a different version; and in that case the story falls to pieces, loses its unity, becomes confused and ugly.

The achievement of this unity, like the achievement of truth, may be the result of a happy accident or of a training which has become effortless. But the deliberate pursuit of it is the deliberate effort to imagine coherently; and it is the presence of this effort that seems to distinguish art in the full sense of the word from dreaming. To dream is to imagine, but not to work at imagining; when we dream, we are doing in a lazy and haphazard way the same thing which in creating a work of art we are doing with critical care and labour. Consequently our dreams now attain beauty, and now give an impression of jarring and idiotic ugliness, and this by no good or bad management on our own part. Yet, though we do not deliberately work at constructing our dreams, they are never entirely formless; and their form is not the result of chance, but the fruit of those activities which we repress and control when we deliberately construct a work of art. Every deliberate activity has, as its negative side, the repression of another activity, which reasserts itself when our active control fails. A dangerous sport involves the repression of fear; and when we fail to maintain the activity of climbing, fighting or the like, our fear rises up and threatens to overcome us. Hence the structure of dreams reveals under analysis the nature of the activities which in full-blown art are repressed; and this is the principle which underlies the practice of psycho-analysis.

But to control our imagination by the deliberate attempt to "imagine out" an object cannot consist in selecting, out of a number of alternatives, something to be imagined. For in that case all the alternatives must be already present to the mind, that is, already imagined. In thinking something out, as Kepler thought out the paths of the planets, we imagine the alternatives and then accept one and reject the rest; but in imagination the first stage does not exist. In making up a tune, we do not try the various notes to see which to put next; we imagine the whole tune, and then, if we are dissatisfied with it, reimagine it afresh with some change which in altering a single note alters the quality of the whole. Hence the will to imagine is a will which does not contemplate alternatives; it is an "immediate" will, a will merely to do what one is doing. And in this way art is the most primitive practical activity, just as it is the most primitive theoretical activity.

§ 6 *The Monadism of Art*

In imagining, we do not contemplate the alternative possible imaginations. It follows that the coherence or unity which is the goal of imagination is a coherence of this individual imagination with itself, and not with any other. So far as it is a successful piece of imagining considered in itself, it is beautiful; and this beauty is quite unaffected by the question whether anybody else or I myself at another time have imagined anything compatible or incompatible with it. In this, imagining is sharply opposed to thinking. To imagine is to isolate the object; to think is to place it in a world of objects with which it is continuous. The coherence of imagination is a merely internal coherence; the coherence of thought is an external coherence, self-transcending as the other is self-contained. If two plays are written about Julius Caesar, presenting incompatible versions of his character, they may both be beautiful; but if two biographies of him are incompatible, they cannot both be true.

The self-transcendence of thought implies that there is in the last resort only one object of thought, namely reality as a whole; within this one object every individual object of thought has its place, conditions every other and is conditioned by them in its turn. The unity of the real world does not cancel or make illusory the plurality of its parts; it is the unity not of an abstract and indivisible unit but of a totality whose very being lies in the diversity of its interrelated parts. Whenever we think of any single thing as real, we are assuming, consciously or unconsciously, the infinite context of reality as a whole; and whenever we speak of reality as a whole we are focusing our thought upon some one part or feature of it, which is emphasized to the exclusion of the rest. Every perception, every judgement of science or history or philosophy, has this twofold aspect.

But there is nothing of this kind in the case of art. One work of art does not imply another; in imagining one work of art we are not implicitly imagining all other works of art, we are ignoring them; and to ignore an imaginary object is simply to condemn that object to non-existence so far as my world is concerned, for my world, as an imaginary world, only exists in my act of imagination. Hence to imagine one work of art is not to deny all others, for that which is denied must simultaneously be imagined; it is simply not to imagine any other, and therefore the world of which, in that act, one is imaginatively aware is a world consisting of this one work of art and nothing else whatever.

Every work of art as such, as an object of imagination, is a world wholly self-contained, a complete universe which has nothing outside it. As soon as the existence of anything else is recognized simultaneously with its own, it no longer exists as a work of art at all, for it is no longer being imaginatively contemplated. This may be expressed by saying that every work of art is a monad, a windowless and self-contained world which mirrors the universe from its own unique point of view, and indeed is nothing but a vision or perspective of the universe, and of a universe which is just itself. Nothing can go into it or come out of it; whatever is in it must have arisen from the creative act which constitutes it.

Nevertheless, if we look at works of art not from the aesthetic point of view but from the historical, we find that there is a plurality of them. The imaginative act as such can never be aware of anyhing but its own self-contained object; but reflection upon this imaginative act reveals it as only one in a system of mutually exclusive or monadic works of art. The historical point of view reveals the existence of an indefinite plurality of these, and is able to detect relations between them: relations of succession, resemblance, dependence, and so forth. Whereas the aesthetic point of view is solely concerned with the appearance of the world as seen from this point, the historical point of view is concerned with the manner in which the observer has arrived at that particular aesthetic point of view. The problem of the genesis of a given work of art is a problem with which art as such has nothing to do; the artist neither knows nor cares whether the work he is now creating is original or imitative, what suggested it, and so forth; but the historian of art is concerned precisely with this problem of genesis. From this genetic point of view it becomes clear that any given work of art is based upon the entire previous experience of the artist; not his artistic experience, but his whole experience; and that it is, historically considered, an attempt to concentrate this whole experience into a single imaginative view of reality. What the artist sees as an absolutely unique creation, the historian sees as another attempt added to the long list of previous attempts to express the meaning of life in a symbolic form. Both the artist and the historian regard the work of art as expressive: but whereas the artist regards it as expressive simply of itself, the historian regards at as expressive of the experiences, now forgotten, which have paved the way for its creation.

To speak of looking at works of art from the aesthetic point of view and from the historical point of view does not imply that what is seen from these two points of view is the same thing. The work of art is seen as a work of art only from the aesthetic point of view: cease to look at it imaginatively, and it ceases to be a work of art: what you are now looking at is not a work of art at all but something different in kind, an historical fact, namely the fact that this particular aesthetic act has occurred. The reflective and historical knowledge that this act has occurred is a different act of consciousness from the act itself, and the objects of these two acts are no less different than the acts themselves.

It will be seen at a later stage of the argument that the aesthetic and reflective points of view are not the exclusive property of the artist and the historian or critic respectively: for, as we shall see, not only are the historian and critic at bottom the same, but the artist is only a conscious and deliberate artist because he is also a critic; and clearly, the critic can only be a critic because he is an artist first and foremost. Hence the monadism of art is a monadism which, establishing itself afresh in every aesthetic act, is broken down afresh by every act of historical or critical reflection: and all actual artistic work consists in the balancing of these two activities.

§ 7 *Art in its Specific Nature:*
Emotionally, as the Enjoyment of Beauty

Every activity is at once pleasant and painful: pleasant in so far as it succeeds in being or doing what it is trying to be or do, painful in so far as it fails. The pleasure and the pain can never be altogether separated; for the effort to do a thing is a mark of insufficient power or skill, and is therefore necessarily painful; where no effort is involved, the activity ceases to have any emotional colouring at all, and is therefore no longer pleasant. Failure and success are relative terms: when we fail, we succeed in doing something, even if it was not the thing we wanted to do: when we succeed, we do what we wanted to do, but that is no longer the thing we now want. Pleasure and pain are therefore two poles of an experience which is the emotional sense of our own activity; they are not distinct experiences, but a given activity may be called pleasant rather than painful so far as we feel ourselves overcoming its difficulties, painful rather than pleasant so far as we feel ourselves strained in the effort to do so.

Pleasure and pain, though in a sense they are the same things wherever they occur, have their own peculiar quality for every specific activity. These specific differences immediately distinguish the pleasure of one kind of experience from that of another, and they are as incapable of being described as of being interchanged. To explain how the pleasure of poetry differs from the pleasure of bathing is as impossible as to explain how red differs from blue. But the specific diversity of pleasures goes much further than this. There is an equally indescribable, and equally unmistakable, difference between the aesthetic pleasure of natural beauty and that of the beauty of art; between the beauty of a pattern and the beauty of a portrait, and so forth. These differences in themselves can only be felt; but they have grounds or conditions which can be described; and an attempt will be made to describe some of these in later chapters.

The presence of an emotional side is universal in all

activity; but its presence is generally thought to be peculiarly necessary, and its function peculiarly central, in
the case of art. No one would, except in joke, define
justice as that which pleases the legal mind, or assert that
the function of mathematical truth is to give pleasure to
mathematicians; but people have seriously maintained
that beauty is that which pleases in a certain way, or
pleases a certain type of mind, or even, simply, pleases;
and it is clear that hedonism, while no doubt just as
unsatisfactory in the philosophy of art as in logic or ethics,
is a great deal more plausible here than elsewhere.

The reason for this is that beauty is not a quality of
objects apprehended by perception, nor yet a concept
grasped by thought; it is an emotional colouring which
transfuses the entire experience of the imagined object.
In a previous section beauty has been defined as imaginative coherence. This coherence is qualitatively, as well as
quantitatively, distinct from the coherence of an object
of thought. Quantitatively, the coherence of imagination
is the coherence of the object with itself, whereas the
coherence of thought is not merely this but also a further
coherence of the object with other objects as parts of a
larger whole. But there is also a qualitative distinction.
The coherence of the object of thought is apprehended
intellectually or discursively as a system of relations between parts each of which can be thought of separately;
the coherence of the object of imagination is intuitively
felt as an incandescence, so to speak, of the whole. It is
only under analysis that this incandescence or emotional
colouring is found to consist in an immediate or intuitive
awareness of relations between the parts of the object.
What is felt as a peculiar thrill, indescribable but easily
recognizable, at the point in the Waldstein Sonata which
a small boy used to call the "moonrise," turns out on

analysis to be the contrast between the key of E major
and that of C in which the sonata began; the thrill is the
fusion of these two keys into a single indivisible experience in which each acquires its significance from the
simultaneous awareness of the other.

This qualitative peculiarity of imaginative coherence,
as a felt quality running through the whole rather than an
articulated system of relations between its parts, results
necessarily from its quantitative peculiarity. In order to
follow out a system of relations in all its detail, one must
be able to think first of one and then of another: to concentrate on one part at a time, and pass on to the next.
When this is done, each part presents itself as the distinct
object of a distinct act of thought; and because the whole
world is implied in the thought of any given object,
therefore, and in the same way, the whole object is implied in the thought of any of its parts. But to imagine a
given object is not to imagine any other; and therefore to
imagine any part of an object is not to imagine the
rest. Hence, from the imaginative or aesthetic point
of view, a work of art is not divisible into parts at all;
that which appears to reflective analysis as a part is
from the aesthetic point of view fused with the rest into
an indivisible whole. The sonnet may be divided into
lines and words, but what is divided is not that imaginative experience which is the sonnet regarded as a work of
art, but something which may by reflection be shown to
be a condition of that experience. This is why a work of
art is always in danger of losing what painters call breadth
through minute attention to detail; as soon as the artist
really concentrates on a detail, the whole has vanished.
Breadth, which means unity, can only be obtained when
each detail is felt not as a part but as a modification of the
whole.

The imaginative activity is therefore one in which the relation between theoretical, practical, and emotional elements is peculiarly close. It is impossible for a scientist to discover a truth without emotion; yet it is easy to distinguish the truth from the emotion of discovering it. But in the case of art this distinction cannot be made. Beauty is present to the mind simply in the form of an emotion. This emotion is bipolar; it is not merely pleasant, but pleasant and painful; and whereas those people who never go very deep into art regard it as a pleasant experience, but one whose pleasure is somewhat trivial and unimportant, those who exert their imaginative powers to the utmost find in that exertion not only a higher and more valuable pleasure but frequent and intense pain. This pain is caused not only by the spectacle of bad art, but equally, though in a different way, by all acute awareness of beauty; so much so that one constantly finds oneself afraid to go to a concert, to read a poem, to look at a very beautiful scene, not from fear of possible ugliness but from fear of too great beauty; and it is this fear that prompts the hatred and suspicion which a respectable mediocrity feels towards the highest art and the greatest splendours of nature.

2 THE FORMS OF BEAUTY

§ 8 *The Forms of Beauty*

The term beauty has hitherto been used in a general sense as a name for that quality of an object in virtue of which it satisfies the claims of the aesthetic spirit. But though this use of the word is legitimate, it requires both defence and modification. We are accustomed to think that some works of art aim not so much at beauty as at sublimity, pathos, humour, tragedy, and so forth. Sometimes we tend to distinguish these from beauty and to say that such and such a picture is sublime but not beautiful, such and such a woman pretty but not beautiful, and so forth; in which case we generally regard beauty not as merely on a level with the rest but as a higher thing, and the thing which all works of art ought ideally to possess; though people sometimes rebel against this view and regard it as no less monstrous to claim that all art should be beautiful than to claim that all art should be comic, thus implying that beauty is one only among a number of species of a genus, aesthetic excellence, for which we have no name. Sometimes, on the other hand, we do not distinguish sublimity, pathos, and the rest from beauty, but only from each other, regarding them as the species of beauty, the various forms into which it is differentiated.

These differences of view are perplexing, and our perplexity increases when we observe that there seem to be as many of these forms of beauty as one chooses to distinguish, and that the methods of defining and classifying them seem to be as arbitrary as their number. And hence it would seem a wholly desirable simplification of the philosophy of art to ignore them altogether; to recognize one and only one form of aesthetic excellence, which may conveniently be called beauty, and to maintain that these forms of beauty are merely arbitrary ways of cutting up and sorting the infinite plurality of beautiful objects—a task whose motives are not aesthetic at all, but merely motives of convenience, as the arrangement of words in a dictionary is a question of convenience and not of philology.

But this proposed simplification, though certainly

itself convenient, is not satisfying. No one thinks that there is any philological significance in the alphabetical arrangement of a dictionary, but every one has always thought that there is some aesthetic significance in the distinction between the sublime and the comic. And it is impossible to explain why a question of convenience in the sorting and cataloguing of words of art should ever have been confused with a question concerning their aesthetic quality. Certain predicates attached to works of art are intended and taken as implying a judgement on their aesthetic quality; others are not. If we call a work of art sublime, or idyllic, or lyrical, or romantic, or graceful, we mean to call attention to something in the character of the work itself, and what we say about it amounts to praise or blame of the artist as such. On the other hand, if we call it a seascape or a villanelle or a fugue we are attaching to it a predicate with no aesthetic significance whatever, and are therefore neither praising it nor blaming it. Some words are used in both ways: thus to call something a tragedy may mean that it has a peculiar kind of aesthetic quality, or merely that it deals with a certain type of subject.

Distinctions of this kind reappear in other fields. For instance, we may attach to actions either predicates which indicate their moral quality or predicates which do not. It is perfectly legitimate to classify an act as an instance of knocking a man down or writing a cheque; but nobody thinks that when we do so, we are in any sense pronouncing upon the moral quality of the act, and nobody would think it necessary for moral philosophy to enter into such classifications. But it would be absurd to seize upon this obvious truth as an excuse for banishing all conceptions from the field of moral philosophy except the one conception of the good, and for maintaining that moral philosophy need not consider distinctions like that between expediency and duty or law and conscience. In the same way, the philosophy of art must steer between the Scylla of attaching falsely aesthetic values to predicates which have no aesthetic intention, merely because they are predicated of works of art, and the Charybdis of denying the existence of distinctions within the one concept of beauty, swallowing up the diversities of the aesthetic spirit in its unity, and reducing itself to the repetition of an empty formula.

The double danger is perhaps due to an excessive confidence in the logic of classification. A genus divides into species in such a way that whatever is in the genus falls in one species and only one. Now if the sublime, the comic, and the rest are species of the beautiful, then every work of art is, first, beautiful, and, secondly, sublime or comic or what not. But sometimes we call a work of art both sublime and comic; and sometimes we say— generally with a suggestion of dispraise—that something is sublime or comic or tragic but not beautiful. To ex- plain the former case away by saying that *Hamlet* is not one work of art but a variety entertainment composed of tragic and comic fragments is to proclaim the bankruptcy of one's theory; to dismiss the latter as a mere freak of language is to confess one's inability to understand what the people who use this language mean.

The beautiful and its various forms are not related either as species of an unnamed genus, or as a genus, beauty, and its species. The highest beauty somehow contains within itself, as subordinate and contributory elements, both the sublime and the comic, and indeed all other forms of beauty; so that these forms appear as parts of a whole, the whole being beauty. But where these elements fall apart, where we get one form in apparent isolation, we do not wholly fail of beauty: the one element constitutes a beauty in itself, but a beauty of a truncated and incomplete kind, beauty at a lower level of development. A good joke is beautiful in its way, and in its way completely beautiful; yet it is only a joke, and this "only" marks an aesthetic shortcoming; its beauty is of a limited and defective kind, so much so that we might hesitate even to call it beautiful at all, but might prefer to say that it was not beautiful, but only comic. But a joke skilfully set in a context of tragedy overcomes this defect. It does not become any funnier, but it becomes beautiful with the beauty of a complete and balanced work of art, a beauty to whose completeness it contributes something vital, and whose completeness, thus achieved, is reflected upon itself.

The forms of beauty, then, are not mutually exclusive forms; indeed they are mutually implicative, and each gains, rather than loses, by fusion with the rest. To argue that sublimity, for instance, cannot be a distinguishable aesthetic predicate because every true work of art turns out on inspection to contain something of the sublime, is to confess oneself the victim of a logical blunder, and to discredit not the concept of sublimity, but the use one is making of the logic of genus and species; it is like arguing that because this table is brown it cannot also be square, unless brownness and squareness are identical.

The following sections are an attempt to distinguish the forms of beauty and to give an account of their mutual implications; but not to do this exhaustively. The parts of a whole cannot be exhaustively enumerated, because within these other parts can always be distinguished *ad infinitum*. All we shall do is to distinguish enough of these forms to exhibit the principle involved in the distinction; while fully recognizing that a closer examination of our pattern at any point would reveal pattern within pattern.

§ 9 *The Sublime*

It is generally said that the sublime has some special connexion with overwhelming power; but what this connexion is, authorities are not agreed. If, as they sometimes seem to imply, a work of art is sublime when it depicts a very powerful thing, and if a natural object is sublime when, in addition to being beautiful, it is also very powerful, then sublimity is not an aesthetic predicate at all, for it marks not a special kind of beauty but a special kind of situation in which beauty may—or may not—be found. But this is not a just account of the way in which the word sublimity is actually used. A picture of an elephant, an express locomotive, a storm at sea, or a great mountain, does not acquire a title to the name sublime merely on account of the scale and power of its subject; nor is it true that the aesthetic feelings with which we regard such powerful things are always and as a matter of course described as sublime feelings. And on the other hand the word is often used in cases where no such power is evident. These facts are generally admitted, and the theory has been modified to meet them by extending the notion of power first to "moral" power, which would permit us to extend the notion of sublimity to the spectacle of weakness and defeat heroically endured, and then to the consciousness of power elsewhere than in the object, as for instance in ourselves or in God. But the real difficulty of the conception lies not in adjusting the definition to the extent of the things defined, but in determining what precisely is meant by power.

It is plain that physical force and bigness, and what is called moral force, have nothing essential to do with sublimity. Any object may be found sublime if approached from the right point of view; just as a beautiful object is not an object having a special kind of shape or colour but an object which the beholder regards imaginatively, so a sublime object is not one possessed in itself of certain attributes but one which the beholder regards with that peculiar modification of the imaginative attitude which stands to sublimity as imagination in the absolute sense stands to beauty. It is in our relation to the object, not in the object considered apart from that relation, that the ground of sublimity must be sought.

That power or force which makes an object sublime can only be its power over us; and not any power, but a specifically aesthetic power, power to make us realize its beauty. Sublimity, therefore, is beauty which forces itself upon our mind, beauty which strikes us as it were against our will and in spite of ourselves, beauty which we accept passively and have not discovered, by a deliberate search for it, in the place where we should expect to find it. Some such feeling of passive acquiescence in a beauty that seems to sweep upon us and overwhelm us from without is never altogether absent from any aesthetic experience, and therefore all beauty has some tinge of sublimity; but the most striking cases of sublimity are those in which this unexpectedness is most marked. Such are cases where our mind has been preoccupied by cares other than aesthetic; where we have been obsessed by fear or desire, or where we have habitually regarded some object as merely useful or merely a nuisance. Thus a person who lives among mountains sees them rather as beautiful than as sublime; but a person who, climbing them in fatigue and in some fear, suddenly becomes conscious of their beauty, which so long as he is wholly absorbed in his climbing he cannot do, sees their beauty as sublimity. So the noise of a bombardment, the buildings of factories and engineering works, a distorted human face, and other things which are generally regarded either as positively ugly or as having no aesthetic character at all, reveal their beauty in the form of sublimity.

The sublime is the first and most elementary form of the beautiful. Sublimity is the mere revelation of beauty as beauty, the inrush of aesthetic experience. At the first moment of its enjoyment, in its absolute novelty, as an absolute creation, all beauty is sublime and nothing else. But conservation is only sustained creation, and that activity whose first fulguration is pure sublimity must continue to be freshly active at every point of its course; and hence all beauty is sustained by a spring of sublimity at its heart.

§ 10 *The Comic*

But the experience of sublimity contains an element of illusion which makes it unstable. The power which is sublimity appears in that experience as belonging to an object which compels us in spite of ourselves to admire it; the object seems to be active, we to be passive. But this is not really the case. The power which we attribute to the object is really our own; it is our own aesthetic activity. The shock of sublimity is the shock of an uprush of imaginative energy within ourselves; and the illusion consists in the fact that we do not feel this energy as our own. No doubt, it is an energy which we could not stifle if we would, for the act by which we would stifle it could only be another manifestation of it, and hence we are not able to choose whether we shall manifest it or not;

but this is not because the power in question is a power outside ourselves, but because it is ourselves.

The sublime object is therefore in something of a false position, or rather we by regarding it as sublime have put ourselves in a false position; we are worshipping an idol whose divine attributes are only the magnified shadow of our own powers. Now this might be discovered reflectively by philosophical analysis; but it may also be discovered intuitively by merely finding that the sublime object, when the first shock of its revelation is over, ceases to impress us as sublime. It is a familiar fact that the experience of sublimity is unstable, and that what we first find sublime we find on further acquaintance perhaps beautiful, perhaps merely pretentious; and this change of attitude, experienced by the aesthetic consciousness and descriptively recorded by psychology, is explained by the conception of sublimity as the first form of beauty, the initiation of an act which, once initiated, must necessarily pass beyond its own starting-point. If then sublimity is the first approximation of the aesthetic experience towards the ideal of beauty, the second approximation must be the correction of the error involved in the first. This error was the ascription of power to the object and of passivity to the beholder; the correction of this must be the recognition that the object owes its sublimity to the observer's act; and the intuitive or non-philosophical form of this recognition will be a feeling of power on one's own part, correlative to a feeling that the object is not in itself the awe-inspiring thing we had fancied it. Where we had exalted the object and abased ourselves, we now exalt ourselves and abase the object.

This change of attitude is the proverbial step from the sublime to the ridiculous. To find an object ridiculous involves a certain contempt of it, just as to find an object sublime involves a certain awe of it; and laughter has sometimes been regarded as a symptom of contempt merely. This is too simple an account of the matter. No one likes being laughed at; but if nature had devised laughter as an instinctive expression of social criticism, she would have produced a very clumsy mechanism for her purpose. The theory of laughter belongs to the philosophy of art; the satisfaction which we find in it is an aesthetic satisfaction, and to this extent the comic is a form of the beautiful. But it is that form of the beautiful in which the aesthetic quality is felt to depend not on the object but on the subject; and therefore a ridiculous object is not necessarily a beautiful object, but may be, and in the cases where the element of ridicule appears in the purest form generally is, an object definitely felt as not beautiful. Hence the comic has often been regarded as a peculiar case of the ugly, an ugliness which does not outrage our aesthetic sensibilities but gives them scope for a peculiar kind of activity. Such a definition is sound as far as it goes, but it fails to account for the fact that we find many things amusing which are far from ugly; the fact that there is a friendly and sympathetic laughter as well as a hostile, a cynical, and a defiant.

The comic is the object of an aesthetic frame of mind which may be called the revolt or reaction against sublimity. The shock with which we discover a beauty dies away: we become familiar with the object, and familiarity breeds a feeling that the beauty which we saw in it was our own work and not due to any real power in the object. The object no longer overawes or impresses us with its beauty, and this release from awe, uprush of positive self-feeling, or, as Hobbes called it, "sudden glory," is what we express by laughter. The pricked bubble of sublimity collapses into ridicule; and we never

in fact laugh without the feeling that something is breaking up, that some tension is relaxed, that some mountain's labour has brought forth a mouse, that something
has failed to justify its pretensions. But a mere collapse
or disappointment is not comic; it must be an aesthetic
collapse, a collapse of the sublime, a collapse of something
that has impressed us not just anyhow, but aesthetically.
And yet to be impressed by anything—an opinionated
man who infects us with the belief in his own knowledge;
a dangerous sea-crossing; an alarm of fire; an angry bull
—has an aesthetic side in which we find that thing sublime; and therefore when the thing in question turns out
not to be formidable, the feeling of sublimity is dissipated in laughter. Hence we tend to laugh at any escape
from danger or anxiety; the child laughs on getting out
of school, and we all have an unregenerate tendency to
laugh when we see another overtaken by a misfortune
which we have ourselves escaped. This is a crude and
barbarous laughter because it is based on forgetting that
we too are subject to the same misfortunes, and that
school will begin again; and these reflexions are apt to
kill our mirth. But they do not kill it outright. There is
a higher type of laughter which remembers our own
frailty, faces our own perils, and yet refuses to be impressed by them; which finds in our own weakness a
source of mirth not because it is weakness but because
we can rise above it. This type of laughter selects for its
object just those things of which we are afraid, such as
sex, death, or God. Here it is not the release from fear
that gives rise to laughter, but the triumph over a fear
of which we are still conscious; we will not allow ourselves to be overcome by pain and misfortune and the
sense of our own littleness and impotence, and therefore
we face pain with a smile and make a joke of our own

feebleness. This laughter is free from barbarity, and tinged with a certain heroism; but it is essentially an act of defiance, and hence it degenerates into cynicism, blasphemy, and obscenity; we are laughing at ourselves, for to blaspheme is to mock not God but our own religious impulses; and this involves despising ourselves and our common human nature. But this self-degradation, this despising of ourselves in order to assert our own superiority over the self we despise, is a self-contradictory attitude, and the laughter which expresses it is a jarring and tuneless mirth. After all, contemner and contemned are one; and the reassertion of this unity is the act by which the defiant laughter of cynicism is mellowed into humour.

The humorous frame of mind is that in which we laugh at a weakness which we no longer feel as contemptible. Rather, we sympathize with it and do not wish it otherwise, but love it for what it is. There is still a sense of our own superiority to the object, a sense of our strength as contrasted with its weakness: without that, there would be no amusement. But this sense of superiority is no longer contemptuous. We have recovered from the shock of realizing that the object is a weak thing, and have resigned ourselves to the certainty that it is so; and therefore humour has in it a note of melancholy, of pessimism, and even at times of despair. Humour is the highest form of laughter, and at the same time it is comedy passing over into tragedy.

§ 11 *The Beautiful*

The sublime and the comic have been taken in the preceding sections as the first and second forms of the beautiful. Each is beautiful, but in an incomplete and one-sided way. In each case there is a discord between the subject and the object which mars the perfection of the aesthetic enjoyment: either the one or the other is unworthy of its correlative, and the result is a lack of balance, an imperfection in the harmony which here, as in every activity, must ideally subsist between subject and object. The disillusionment of laughter is the end of an illusion, but it is itself another illusion, equal and opposite. To overcome both illusions would be to attain the stability in which alone the mind can present to itself a truly beautiful object. But one illusion has already been overcome; and it only remains to overcome the other.

The negative illusion of ridicule has no function except as a counterblast to the positive illusion of sublimity: and therefore, when it has done its work, it exhausts itself for very lack of work to do. It is only in the actual collapse of sublimity that ridicule can exist; when the sublimity has effectively collapsed, the ridicule has consumed its fuel and burnt itself out. A person who has thoroughly eradicated from his mind that false awe of an object which makes him see it as sublime no longer laughs at it.

The cancelling-out of these opposites brings us back in a sense to our starting-point. But it is not a question of mathematics, in which 1 added to —1 makes 0, but of actual experience, in which a movement and a counter-movement leave us enriched by something through which we have lived, and enable us, or rather compel us, to take up a new attitude towards the same starting-point. Once more, we find ourselves impressed by the sublimity of the object; but now we anticipate the collapse of this sublimity into ridicule; we feel the collapse immanent within the sublimity, and so experience both at once instead of trying to maintain the one by itself till the other forces itself upon us in a revulsion of feeling.

Had they been mere contradictories this would have been impossible; had each been nothing but the negation of the other, no synthesis could have been even attempted. But they have this in common, that each is the apprehension of an object which is in some sense beautiful; and what cancels out is not their whole nature but only the complementary illusions which prevented each from being the full apprehension of a fully beautiful object. The synthesis of the sublime and the comic therefore gives us the beautiful in the full sense of the word.

The relation of the sublime and the comic to the beautiful is not exactly that of parts to a whole, just as it is not exactly that of species to a genus, though it resembles both these relations. In their isolation each is not a multilated portion of beauty but a beauty, though an inferior and disturbed beauty; whereas in the relation of whole and part, if all the parts are not present the whole is not present even in a modified degree. And in their synthesis each does not so much supplement the other as negate the other; each loses its peculiar character, and the two thus sink their difference in what is now an identity; whereas the parts of a whole are merely juxtaposed externally, each remaining wholly itself in order to make up what the other lacks. Thus in true beauty there is always present not so much sublimity itself as a transmuted form of sublimity; the mind is not so much overwhelmed with the shock of an unexpected glory as touched to a calm solemnity, a hush in which it hears the voice of the authentic divinity. And there is also present not so much a frankly comic element as an element of sublimated comedy, laughter softened into that smile with which we all naturally contemplate beauty.

Between these two poles of sublimity and comedy lies the whole of that experience which is the contemplation of perfect beauty. When this experience is attained, but attained with a certain lack of clearness and fixity, the mind seems to oscillate between the two poles, on the point of lapsing now into the sublime and now into the comic, but always reacting in time against the threatened obsession and passing over to the opposite pole. Very great works of art are produced by this oscillation; the comic sculptures that incrust a medieval cathedral and the comic scenes that punctuate Elizabethan tragedy are marks not of a frivolity which is incapable of the high seriousness of sublime art, but of a mental balance which will not fall into the pompous pretentiousness of the un-relieved sublime or the cynical triviality of the purely comic, but displays the security of its grasp on true beauty by repeatedly touching first one and then the other of its limits. And a balance of the same kind is achieved when we laugh at a sublime work of art merely because it is sublime and not comic. Seriousness itself is funny be-cause the mind of the beholder, in order to retain its own aesthetic balance, imports into its contemplation of a sublime object just that element of comedy which the object lacks; and thus preserves itself from being engulfed in its sublimity. In this sense, and in this sense only, the "sense of humour" is symptomatic of a "sense of propor-tion," and the man who laughs shows himself a healthy and well-balanced man.

But this compensatory transition from one pole to the other, even in its highest form, where the artist himself in his own single person vibrates between the two poles, is an imperfect enjoyment of the beautiful; it is rather a protest against two false ideals than an embodiment of the true. Hence there is felt to be a certain discord be-tween the solemnity of the cathedral's structure and the ribaldry of its ornament; and the "comic relief" of the old drama is felt by all critics to demand explanation. In such an oscillation between the two poles, the two remain separate; their difference is still emphasized, and the single experience which was to be born of their union remains an unfulfilled promise. The highest art of all no longer vibrates in this way; instead of leaping from one extreme to the other, it has come to rest in the centre.

The mark of this repose is a feeling which can best, perhaps, be described as one of intimacy with the object. The sublime and the comic are alike in this, that the object is held off at arm's length, looked up to in the one case, looked down upon in the other. The mind, in both cases alike, feels itself incommensurate with its object; the power which generates the aesthetic experience is felt as flowing either from object to subject, exciting beauty in a mind incapable of creating it for itself, or from subject to object, conferring beauty on something which in itself does not possess it. The question has sometimes been raised, whether beauty is "objective" or "subjective," by which is meant, whether it belongs to the object and is by it imposed on the mind by brute force, or whether it belongs to the mind and is by it imposed on the object irrespective of the object's own nature. The only meaning so strange a question can have, is whether the sublime or the comic is the true and only form of the beautiful. For real beauty is neither "objective" nor "subjective" in any sense that excludes the other. It is an experience in which the mind finds itself in the object, the mind rising to the level of the object and the object being, as it were, preadapted to evoke the fullest expression of the mind's powers. The experience of beauty is an experience of utter union with the object; every barrier is broken down, and the beholder feels that his own soul is living in the object, and that the object is unfolding its life in his own heart. Hence arises that absence of constraint, that profound sense of content-ment and well-being, that characterizes the experience of real beauty. We feel that it is "good for us to be here"; we are at home, we belong to our world and our world belongs to us.

But that is a merely psychological description of the experience. The feeling which we thus describe has a ground, and this ground can be made explicit by re-flexion on the feeling. The aesthetic activity is the activity of imagination; and imagination creates its own object. Now the experience of sublimity is an act of imagination, and therefore creative of its own object; but in this ex-perience itself we feel as if the object were evoking the act. We are—always in terms of feeling, not in terms of philosophical theorizing—precisely inverting the true position, and erecting into a creator the object which in that very act we have created. Hence the experience of sublimity is an illusion not in the sense that it is a false philosophical theory, but in the sense that it is a feeling whose implications, when we reflect on them, are found to contain a false philosophical theory. This implicit error is implicitly corrected by the transition from the sublime to the comic, but only partly corrected. Again in terms of feeling, to ridicule an object is to regard its sublimity as imaginary, but to regard it, as a thing in itself, as not imaginary. We have stripped the object of its aesthetic quality, and left it naked and contemptible. But this stripped object is in point of fact still an aesthetic object, and therefore an object of imagination: it is an object which we have first created and then degraded, and at which therefore we have no right to laugh. We began by making ourselves an idol and worshipping it; we go on, when our prayers are unanswered, to flog it; the one attitude is as unreasonable as the other. To recover from both forms of unreason is to remember that the idol was made by ourselves to be the expression of our own thought; and the intuitive awareness of this is the feeling of intimacy between our mind and the object which is simply our mind made visible to itself.

This does not imply that the only person who can truly enjoy the beauty of anything is the philosopher who knows that the object is the creature of his own imagination. To enjoy beauty is an imaginative act, not a reflective; and the object of imagination cannot possibly become an object to philosophical thought. The imaginary can only be imagined: if we are to philosophize, we must philosophize not about the imaginary but about the real, not about the object of aesthetic experience but about the act that generates that object. But the enjoyment of beauty, as distinct from sublimity, does presuppose something beside the pure act of imagination: it presupposes the ability to learn from experience, to react differently to a given situation because a similar situation has developed in a particular way in the past.

3 *THE BEAUTY OF NATURE*

§ 12 *The Imaginary Object and the Real Object*

It has already been shown (§ 3) that to call an object imaginary is to express one's indifference as to whether it is real or not. If this is so, and if to imagine an object is to find it beautiful, there is no difficulty in the fact that we find real objects, whether natural objects or works of art, beautiful; for it is just as possible to look imaginatively at these as it is to look imaginatively at objects which exist solely in our own imagination. It is therefore perfectly indifferent, as regards the beauty of an object, whether it is imaginary in the narrower sense of the word or real, and, if real, whether it is a natural object or a work of art. Of these distinctions the aesthetic activity ought to take no cognizance; they belong to the region of reflective thought, not to the region of art. The artist, as artist, ought to look upon these different types of object with precisely the same feelings, and leave it to the philosopher to discriminate between them.

This is the position which would seem to follow necessarily from the general conception of art as imagination. That there is a certain amount of truth in it is undeniable. It is true that an object, whatever else may be said about it, is only beautiful to a person who looks at it imaginatively, and that the kind of beauty which he finds there depends on the intensity and character of his own imaginative activity. It is also true that the aesthetic act is not an act of perception and therefore does not and cannot either assert or deny the reality of its object, and is still less able to assert that its object has come into existence in one kind of way or in another.

But the fact remains that all artists are in the habit of distinguishing natural from artistic beauty, not as one and the same thing found in objects between which philosophical reflection is forced to distinguish, but as two things which are aesthetically distinguishable. Just as it does not take a physicist to decide that something is sublime, so it does not take a philosopher to decide that something has that peculiar kind of beauty which is called natural beauty. The force of the sublime is not physical energy but aesthetic impressiveness; and in the same way the distinction between natural beauty and artistic beauty is not a metaphysical distinction, irrelevant to the artist as such, but a distinction between two kinds of aesthetic experience. Both the natural object and the work of art present themselves to the artist himself as real and not merely imaginary: their reality enters into his aesthetic experience as a constituent element, giving it a quality of its own, and their different origin further differentiates this quality.

But before discussing the distinction between natural and artistic beauty it is necessary to raise the question why the purely imaginative activity of art should ever come to regard its object as real: that is, as independent of its own imaginative act. The paradox lies in the fact that whereas imagination is by definition unconcerned with the reality of its object, it includes one particular type of experience in which it regards its object as essentially real; in which that very distinction which lies outside the competence of imagination appears somehow within imagination itself, not in the form of an assertion—for imagination can never assert—but in the form of a feeling which colours the quality of the imaginative act.

The principle by appeal to which this paradox can be explained is one which made its first appearance at the close of the last section. It was there pointed out that the transition from the antithesis of the sublime and the comic to the beautiful could only be affected by a mind possessed of the capacity to learn from experience. A new and unique aesthetic experience was thus generated by a principle which was not itself aesthetic: for there is only one aesthetic principle, namely imagination: and yet the attitude of imagination to its own object is affected by this non-aesthetic principle. But the mere capacity to

learn by experience is not the only non-aesthetic principle which may introduce a new quality into the aesthetic experience itself.

§ 13 *Inspiration*

It may be doubted whether we ever imagine without also
thinking. In most cases of dreaming, the objects of our
dream-consciousness are merely imaginary; but in point
of fact we do in dreams make a distinction between
reality and unreality, though as a rule we make it
wrongly, and take for real what is only imaginary. In our
waking imaginations we sometimes know that we are
only imagining, and sometimes wrongly think that we are
not. But there seems to be no case in which we make no
judgement whatever as to whether we are imagining or
not, in other words, whether the immediate object of our
consciousness is a merely imaginary object or a real object; and in many cases it is certainly true that when we
are engaged in the aesthetic activity we know that we are
so engaged. Indeed this must be so in all deliberately-
controlled imagining, in all that we generally call art;
for the will to imagine implies the consciousness that we
are imagining.

The artist, then, is always doing two things: imagining
and knowing that he is imagining. His mind is as it were
a twofold mind and has before it a twofold object: as
imagining, he has before him the imagined object; as
thinking, he has before him his own act of imagining
that object. He knows, and without this he could not be
an artist, that he is aesthetically active; but he does not
understand the relation between this activity and the
other activities which go to make up his nature, for he is
not a philosopher. He thinks of himself as imagining but

he does not think of himself as thinking; yet he is thinking, and so far his self-knowledge is an incomplete and
misleading self-knowledge. The artist, as artist, imagines:
as thinker, he watches himself imagining and by this
watching makes it possible to concentrate himself on the
task of imagining. The thinking self controls the imagining self and makes the difference between a random
dreaming and the deliberate imagination of art. Yet
though the thinking self controls the imagining self, the
artist does not know that this is so; for he is only conscious
that he is imagining, not that he is thinking; and
therefore he knows that something is controlling his
imaginative activity—something other than that activity itself—but does not know that this something is
his own thought.

The consciousness that one's imagination is controlled
by some power other than itself must be distinguished
from the quite different feeling of passivity which characterizes the experience of the sublime. In contemplating
natural beauty, we feel our faculties as adequate to apprehend the object, and the object as adequate to satisfy
the demands of our faculties. The power which controls
the imagination is felt to be, as it really is, a spiritual
activity transcending the imagination but somehow akin
to it: and in so far as the artist thinks of himself as all
imagination, he thinks of this power as a spiritual activity
transcending his own personality, a power which inspires
him to imaginations which his own strength could never
achieve. Of this inspiring power he feels himself to be
the passive mouthpiece.

The inspiring power whose presence is felt by the
aesthetic consciousness is in some sense a god; and therefore this feeling of inspiration might be thought a religious rather than an aesthetic feeling, or at least a point

of transition from art to religion. But this would be an error. Religion begins when the mysterious powers which work upon human life are identified and named; that is to say, when the centre of interest is no longer the effect produced by a force but that force itself. To feel oneself inspired, *pati deum,* is not religion but the raw material of religion; the religious consciousness is one which has overcome this sheer passivity and has dared to inquire what the force that has possessed it is. Religion does not merely "suffer" God, it "walks with" God, holds some kind of communion with him, knows his name. And the aestheic consciousness has no name for the power which inspires it; it has a name only for the experience of being possessed by this power.

§ 14 *Nature*

The belief that one is inspired takes its rise not in the pure act of imagination but in the thought by which one is conscious of oneself as imagining. It might be inferred that this belief could not, as it were, get inside the imagination and colour its activity, but would remain a thing of the intellect, an error—so far as it is an error—which, as thinkers, we make about our aesthetic experience, but which for that very reason cannot affect this experience itself. This would imply that imagination and thought are so far independent of one another that we can think what we please and leave the course of our imaginations unaltered. But every act of imagination is an imaginative reflection or resultant of the man's whole experience, and this experience includes his own thought about his own imaginative activity. If, in so far as he thinks, he recognizes that his imagination is controlled by an activity higher than itself, this recognition must leave its mark on his imagination in the form of a feeling of "givenness" which characterizes its awareness of its object.

Thus the feeling of "givenness" which at first sight seems to contradict the very definition of imagination is really a consequence of that definition; and to suppose that imagination ought to imply an awareness of the object's character as imaginary is to confuse imagination with the philosophical understanding of imagination. It is just because art is art and not philosophy that the artist, whose business is to imagine and not to understand, feels his object as something independent of his imagining it.

The term nature, in whatever context it is used, bears a negative sense. It always indicates a limit of our own activity. Human nature is that which we cannot alter by moral or legislative effort; the forces of nature are those forces which we can only control by obeying them; natural laws and natural rights are those which exist whether human beings recognize them or not. The nature of anything is that which we must accept as an absolute datum; but this datum is correlative to an activity of our own. A starting-point has meaning only with reference to something that starts there: to say that we cannot alter the nature of a thing implies that there is something about it which we can and do alter. Therefore the idea of nature arises as the negative counterpart of the idea of activity, and every kind of activity has its counterpart in a distinct kind of nature. Thus nature in the aesthetic sense is that which we find ourselves under the necessity of imagining, as the starting-point or datum for any further act of imagining which feels itself to be a free act. But as, in perceiving, we feel everything that we perceive to be a natural object, and as, in thinking, the scientist feels every object of his thought to be a part of nature, so, in imagining, the artist feels every object of his imagination to be nature. In all these cases alike the cognitive activity feels its object to be independent of it and set over against it as a limit to its own freedom; though in all these cases the question may be raised by philosophy, whether this feeling is not in some sense an illusion, and whether the object may not in reality be in some sense constituted by the very act which apprehends it.

That this is so in the case of imagination has already been shown. And therefore the feeling of givenness would appear, in this case at least, to be an illusion. But even if it is an illusion, it is a genuine feeling, one which actually enters into the imaginative experience and must be accepted for a fact by any account of that experience. Morever it has been shown in the foregoing analysis to be a necessary fact, a feature which the imaginative activity is bound to develop. If then it is an illusion, it is a necessary illusion; and that is a way of saying that it is not altogether an illusion. In general, this sense of givenness is the finite mind's awareness of its own finitude. A mind that was wholly finite could not be aware that it was finite; where finitude is known it is transcended. But where it is not explicitly or philosophically known but merely felt as the emotional background of an experience, it is not explicitly transcended; there is only a pledge that it can be transcended.

Hence the feeling of givenness in virtue of which the object of imagination is felt as real, as nature, is, properly considered, not an illusion at all, but the imaginative awareness of a profound truth. The artist, in virtue of this feeling, is aware that he is not the idle singer of an empty day, a teller of tales whose only justification is that they are good tales. On the surface, his work is a mere play of fancies; but behind this surface it is quick with a hidden truth, a meaning that goes far beyond what is explicitly said. The artist does not know this meaning; it is for him a mystery hidden behind the imagery that expresses it, a spirit at once revealed and concealed by the visible garment that it wears: but he feels its presence, and this feeling is the sense of inspiration; he traces the pattern in the garment, and this garment is nature.

All this the artist feels as an integral part of his aesthetic experience. He does not, so far as he is an artist, think it out philosophically; he does not even state it as a religious creed. It is present to him simply in the form of a peculiar emotional colouring in the object of his imagination. This emotional colouring would not be experienced at all unless the artist was capable of thinking as well as of imagining. If there could be a mind purely imaginative and devoid of all intellectual faculties, such a mind would be an artist, but its artistic experience would be altogether innocent of the feeling that its object was no mere fiction but a symbol of truth. But though these feelings have their source in thought, they are, as feelings, part and parcel of the aesthetic experience; and necessarily so, because the imaginative faculty and the intellectual cannot in fact exist separately.

§ 15 *The Beauty of Nature*

Because nature is a negative term, it always presupposes its corresponding positive. Nature in the aesthetic sense presupposes the aesthetic activity, and is the negation of this activity as felt by the activity itself. To call an object nature is to express the feeling that it is not in any sense the fruit of our own activity. Hence all beauty is natural beauty so far as it belongs to an object of which we feel ourselves not to be the makers. Whether we are really its makers or not is beside the point; the question is simply what in the actual aesthetic experience we feel to be the relation between ourselves and the object. All beauty is natural beauty if and when we feel thus passively towards it. The object and our awareness of it are felt to be in perfect harmony with each other; but within this harmony there is a distinction between feeling that the object is presented to the aesthetic activity, and feeling that the aesthetic activity, whether in myself or anoher, has created the object; this is the distinction between the enjoyment of natural beauty and the enjoyment of the beauty of art.

The enjoyment of natural beauty is imagination unaware of its own creativity. When imagination discovers its own power of creating objects for itself, it feels itself as art in the fullest sense of the word, and its objects as works of art. Before this discovery, it feels itself as passively contemplating a ready-made nature. But the discovery is not a philosophical conception, it is a discovery made empirically, and therefore recognized in certain cases and not extended to other cases. Hence the distinction between the tang of two different feelings, the feeling of aesthetic receptivity and the feeling of aesthetic creativity, tends to be misinterpreted as a distinction between two species of beautiful objects. The result of such a misinterpretation is the attempt to classify beauties by dividing them into the two mutually-exclusive groups of natural and artistic; and the failure of any such attempt soon becomes evident. It is absurd to ask whether a given object, considered in itself and out of all relation to the imaginative act which apprehends it, is an instance of natural or artistic beauty; and no less absurd to assume, as any such classification must assume, that we take up the same imaginative attitude towards all objects which can be placed in the same class.

Nature is the antithesis not of my private or personal activity but of activity as such; and therefore that object is felt as nature which is felt as the limit or negation of the apprehending activity in general. In order to be aware of any beauty as natural beauty, I must be aware of myself as man; and then the beauty of nature will present itself as the beauty of the non-human world. So far as I am aware of myself, not merely as man in the abstract, but as man in a special aspect, nature will mean to me not the bare negation of humanity but the negation of this special aspect of humanity. Hence natural beauty presents itself in different forms correlative to the aspects of his own life which mostly deeply affects the observer's consciousness. Some of these will be considered in the following section.

All these forms have certain common characteristics. Nature is sometimes called the art of God; and the phrase admirably describes the actual experience, though it is couched in religious language which that experience would not itself naturally use. It implies what in that experience we always feel, that nature is impeccable. Nothing in nature is ugly; when we deny that a natural object is beautiful we are reflecting not upon it but upon ourselves. As such, every natural object is equally beautiful; God takes as much pleasure in the turbot and the hippopotamus as in the nightingale and the lion; his handiwork is a sufficient guarantee of perfection, and if we fail to see that perfection the fault is our own. This follows necessarily from the feeling of passivity: that feeling implies that beauty is everywhere around us in endless profusion, and that all we have to do is to accept

what is given us. Natural beauty has no opposite: it is
either seen or not seen. This gives it a peculiar quality of
immediacy or spontaneity. It is something for which no
one has worked, something that has come absolutely and
exquisitely right by no effort, but by a pure act of divine
grace. The lilies take no trouble over their clothes, and
for that very reason their clothes are perfect. The mountain is beautiful because no one has built it, the forest
because no one has planted it, the snowflake because no
silversmith has touched it with hammer and file; the effortless immediacy of nature is in every case not something accidental to its beauty but the very heart of its
beauty. The primrose of the rock is not both beautiful
and not in a rock-garden; its not being in a rock-garden
is the beauty of it. If art could so exactly reproduce a
natural object that the eye could not detect the imposture, the reproduction, as soon as it was known to be a
reproduction, would lose just that peculiar beauty which
its natural archetype would possess. And in the same way
nature is spoilt by adorning it; to gild the lily, to pinch
and tattoo the human body, to plant a wild landscape
with garden flowers, is to destroy the natural beauty of
the object by interfering with this spontaneity. The same
thing happens if the object is disturbed with no intention
of adorning it, but either with another motive or in
absence of mind: a railway or a quarry destroys the
beauty of a mountain not by suggesting thoughts of utility but simply by cutting up the spontaneous flow of its
lines; our joy in the beauty of a red toadstool is turned
to disgust when we find the toadstool to be a Victoria
plum dropped by a passer-by, not because we dislike
plums or passers-by but because we had been enjoying
the spontaneity of what we took to be nature's colour-
scheme.

Natural beauty is thus beauty in its immediacy, a beauty whose special quality is its freedom from effort, from the attempt to realize something unrealized. There is the same difference between this effortless perfection and the result of artistic labour that there is between the goodness of a person who seems to do right by instinct, and that of one who does right by struggling with his temptations. Nature's song is the song of innocence: art's the song of experience.

§ 16 *The Forms of Natural Beauty*

No aesthetic purpose would be served by a classification of natural beauties. The games of 'animal, vegetable, or mineral', and 'earth, air, fire, and water' have no place in the philosophy of art. But though an attempt to enumerate the various classes of object in which natural beauty may be found is of necessity both unsuccessful and unprofitable, there is within natural beauty a distinction of a different kind; a distinction not between objects but between aesthetic points of view. Natural beauty in general is the beauty of an object which is felt to be the negation of the activity which contemplates it. According as man's self-consciousness undergoes any modification, that which he feels as his own opposite must undergo a parallel modification. In so far as he feels himself merely as man, nature will mean to him that which is not human. When he feels himself not merely as man but as civilized man, nature will be extended so as to include not only the non-human world but the world of human life in its uncivilized state; and the definition of "uncivilized" will vary with the definition of "civilized." When he feels himself to be an artist, nature will be further extended to include even human life at his own level of civilization, so far as it is not inspired by consciously aesthetic motives. Thus, man conscious of himself as man finds natural beauty in the sea and the wind and the stars; man conscious of himself as civilized finds the same type of beauty in primitive human societies and their products: man conscious of himself as an artist finds the same type of beauty in machinery and other utilitarian products of civilization. The type of beauty involved in all these three cases is the same: it is the beauty of contrast between the spectator and his object, the beauty of that which is beautiful because it was not designed to be beautiful: in a word, the immediate beauty of nature. But the three cases represent three very different points of view. The taste which craves an object utterly remote from man is offended by the evidences of even the most primitive human activity; it regards its object as desecrated if the landscape contains a single human figure, the seascape a single sail. The second frame of mind finds nothing incongruous in a nature modified by man, so long as the human influences are relatively primitive: the cottage, the tilled land, the old-fashioned town, fit into the beauty of naure without a jar, and for this frame of mind there is on the one hand something bleak and unsatisfying about the savagery of the purely natural world, while on the other it is offended by the railway, the factory, the steamship, and similar marks of industry. The third frame of mind is as dissatisfied with the spectacle of primitive man as the second is with untouched nature; it regards the picturesque town and the rural countryside as insipid, and takes the same delight in the clean design of an express locomotive or a heavy gun that the first frame of mind takes in the modelling of a mountain and the articulation of a tree. Of these three attitudes, the first is the presupposition and basis of the others; it is perpetuated in the second, because the enjoyment of scenery as such is in this second frame of mind not negated but regarded as by itself un-satisfying and in need of a supplement; and it is still present in the third, because the beauty of utilitarian inventions is felt to depend upon the principle of con-quering natural forces by obeying them. These three phases of natural beauty must now be considered in turn.

(a) The first and most primitive is the beauty of pure nature. Pure nature, or nature as such, is defined by con-trast with man as such. Man, conscious of his own activity, finds himself confronted by a world which is not the fruit of that activity, and the feeling of this givenness, this re-moteness from his own interference, constitutes the special character of natural beauty in this sense. The sun and moon and stars, the mountain and the forest, the flowers and animals, the birds and fishes, the sea and the river, the clouds and wind and rain, all have this beauty of wildness. This feeling is not the fruit of a sophisticated civilization, except in the sense that to be self-conscious is already to be sophisticated. It is not because the world is too much with us that we turn to the beauty of wild things; unless indeed the world simply means ourselves. The primitive savage feels this beauty no less keenly than the town-dweller; primitive literature is no less full of its echoes than the literature of an industrial age; and the nature-worship which is especially characteristic of un-civilized races represents a religious development of precisely this feeling for the aesthetic power of wild na-ture. To people the desert with naiads and oreads, spirits of the cloud and the lightning, gods of vegetable growth and stellar movement, is to betray the universality and depth of the feeling for pure natural beauty.

This feeling is dissipated by finding traces of human action in the natural object. When the wild is tamed, the beauty of its wildness disappears; and hence the advance of human power over nature always tends to restrict the scope and opportunities of this frame of mind. As the desert is cultivated, as the river is bridged and diked, as the mountain is quarried for stone and the forest felled for timber, they cease to evoke the response which was due to their defiance of human control; and since these changes result necessarily from man's self-consciousness, the same gift which is the source of his enjoyment of their beauty is the source of his progressive destruction of that enjoyment. But there are always things which preserve their wildness; man cannot leave his mark upon the stars, and however he may defile the wind with smoke and the sea with oil, their own elemental energy, like the energy of vegetable growth, breaks in upon him unimpaired. There is still, and there must always be, an infinite field for the enjoyment of pure natural beauty.

But as man becomes more reflective and learns to see more in himself, pure nature ceases to satisfy him. The savage possibly enjoys it more than the civilized man; certainly among ourselves it is the young and the less reflective that find wild nature most lastingly satisfying. Not that any of us lose our joy in it; but as our own self-consciousness becomes deeper we tend to supplement it by additions and modifications which would have offended us at an earlier stage of our development, but which we now feel as enriching instead of destroying nature.

(b) These additions are based upon the principle that nature, to be beautiful, need no longer be wholly untouched by man; and that human interference, so far from impairing its beauty, may in certain circumstances even enhance it. To the eye which delights in pure natural beauty, the wild flower is delightful because it is in its right place; it fits into its surroundings, it has grown inevitably out of the influences of soil and climate, and this inevitability, though we may know nothing of geology and botany, is actually felt as an organic unity between the flower and the country in which it grows. But this very same unity may be felt in the case of human products. The cottage, built of oak beams or of bricks or of stone, seems to express the character of the soil on which it stands, and is beautiful not because it is built in one material rather than another, but because it is built in the material of which the landscape itself is built. The footpath across the moor adds to the beauty of the moor because it records the fashion in which men have picked their way across the country, and therefore subtly emphasizes the modelling and texture of that country. The arable lands and the meadows bring into relief, by their respective character, the varying qualities of the soil, no less than does the natural vegetation. Even the people, after living for generations in contact with nature, seem infected with the flavour of nature; they walk like shepherds, their eyes are the eyes of hillmen, their speech has modelled itself upon their occupations as their occupations have modelled themselves upon the land.

Even apart from the ways in which this human life has grafted itself upon nature and acquired something of nature's quality, it is felt to be in its own right a possessor of natural beauty. The manners and customs of such a society seem a kind of natural law, by contrast with the fashions of a sophisticated society; for they are the direct and unreflective expression of an immemorial tradition, which the individual is no more free to disregard than the individual rose is free to disregard the compulsion which makes it a rose. We take a peculiar pleasure in the spectacle of this life, its daily routine, its ceremonial of feast and holiday; a pleasure which is based on the feeling that there is here no conscious choice, no explicit question of whether a given act shall or shall not be done, a given costume worn or not worn. Thus we enjoy a Provençal carnival not because, considered as a work of art, it is above criticism, but because it is taken by everybody concerned as a matter of course; and if some one got up a carnival at Blackpool we should feel, not that it would necessarily be worse done, but that however well it was done it would lack the one thing that makes a carnival attractive. It would be like hiring a man to jodel on the Keswick coach.

This peculiar type of natural beauty is not confined to rural life; it is equally found in the life of towns, so far as these towns are felt to be remote from the bustle and sophistication of our own modern town-life. If a name for it is necessary, one might perhaps, though not without hesitation, make use of the word picturesque; for that word clearly denotes a form of natural beauty, since the essence of the picturesque is the spectator's sense of a gulf between the object and his own habitual surroundings and activities, and at the same time the word is applied indifferently to natural objects and to the life and works of man.

The love of natural beauty is often regarded as a peculiarly modern thing, a fruit of our urban and industrial civilization. If nature means the picturesque, this is true; or rather, it is true that the industrializing of our civilization has produced a new form of the picturesque, and has concentrated our feeling for natural beauty upon the spectacle of a rural society living in the pursuit of traditional arts and deeply rooted in a landscape which has in part created it and in part been created by it. Such a society is the pit whence we were digged; it is what we all were before the industrial revolution; and when that event had divorced us from this state of things, our civilization began to feel its own industrialism as artificial and the pre-industrial society of the countryside and the little town as natural and, therefore, as endowed with all the peculiar qualities of natural beauty. This feeling created for itself a mouthpiece in Wordsworth, and for the last century and a half the movement announced by Wordsworth has steadily increased in depth and strength. To this can be traced all the modern interest in ballad-literature and folk-song and peasant arts, the taste for cottage architecture, the instinctive reversion of town-bred people to country pursuits, and the attempt to preserve beautiful places from being trampled out of existence by the overflow of town life.

This movement is by far the most important fact in the aesthetic life of our own country at the present day; to say nothing of other countries; for the earlier rise of industrialism in England led to an earlier development of this feeling among ourselves. People who think that the aesthetic life means cultivating poetry and endowing opera-houses are apt to believe that the English of to-day are an inartistic race, and even to feel puzzled by the fact that Shakespeare, Purcell, and Turner were Englishmen. But the aesthetic energy of modern England is concentrated upon a very widespread and very profound love of nature, and nature for us means what it meant to Wordsworth, not the opposite of man but the opposite of industrialized man. According to our means and our education, we prefer Hampstead Heath or the Cornish coast or the Lake District or Switzerland; but the same impulse drives us all. Our first thought, when holiday-time comes round, is to flock into the country; and we do this not in order to stretch our legs or to repair our health, but in order to enjoy the beauty of the country. If we wanted exercise, we could get it in our towns, like the ancient Greeks; if we were anxious about our health, we could live more healthily all the year round; but we will forgo exercise and overwork ourselves for the most part of our time in order to see the country from a cottage-window at week-ends, or travel from Manchester to Bournemouth and back in a motor coach, or take the steamer to Rothesay, or go to the Tirol for a month. Every class of society does these things, and if we were not obsessed by the false philosophy of art which we have inherited from nineteenth-century aestheticism, we should see that in all classes alike the motive of these vast mass-movements is purely aesthetic.

It is the more important that we should understand the basis and the limitations of this motive. It is some-times supposed that to find a primitive society beautiful implies a sentimental blindness to its defects; that to discover that the people whom one regards as picturesque are unhappy, underfed, spiteful, lazy, and immoral destroys the sense of their beauty. But this is not so. It is not when the village girl drowns her illegitimate baby that she ceases to be beautiful, but when she dresses in what she takes to be fashionable clothes; it is not when the cottage becomes leaky or verminous that it loses its picturesqueness, but when it is adorned with china cats and fortified with a corrugated iron roof. Nor is it a valid criticism of this attitude to point out—what is quite true—that it objects to the railway and the gasometer because they are innovations, but does not object to the enclosed fields, the two-storied cottages, the metalled country lanes, and the stone churches, which were equally innovations in their time. The lover of the picturesque is no blind *laudator temporis acti*. He does not praise beauty because it is traditional, but tradition because it has created beauty; he loves the cottage and hates the gasometer quite consistently, because the cottage falls into its place in the landscape and the gasometer does not.

But it is true that the love of the picturesque is a self-contradictory attitude and one which is bound to destroy what is loves by the very fact that it loves it. The motor-coach that ruins the beauty of the country lane and the hotel that destroys the picturesqueness of the Alpine village have been created and launched on their work of destruction by the love of what they have destroyed. It is because Wordsworth has taught so many people to see beauty in the Lake District that the Lake District which he enjoyed no longer exists; the same thing has happened in Switzerland, on the Riviera, and wherever beauty of this peculiar kind has been discovered and enjoyed. The discovery is made by some adventurous spirit who penetrates to a place where the scenery is untouched by the hard lines of road and railway, the architecture unspoilt by the intrusion of hotels and villas, the people unaffected in their manners, primitively hospitable, and picturesquely clad without self-consciousness; and thereupon writes to his friends, with Sophoclean irony, "this place is perfect; no one ever comes here." But, unseen by himself, he has gone there; he is already the one blot on that landscape, the one note out of tune in that pastoral symphony; he is the thin end of the wedge, and his own praises drive the wedge home. He is the spy sent out in advance by the mob of trippers and bank-holiday makers, and he has no choice but either to encourage others to continue the work of destruction which he has begun, or to incur the just reproach of wishing to prevent others from sharing in what he regards as the most precious of pleasures.

This is why those who live in beautiful places for the sake of their beauty are jealous lovers, and hostile towards all who wish to follow them. They fight, and cannot help fighting, against the incursion of railways and motor roads, against the increase of building and the organization of cheap trips; but they are traitors to their own cause, for they are themselves nothing but squatting trippers, centres of infection where the artificial life which they represent has broken through its barriers into the picture which they wish to enjoy. Their own houses and gardens are already a fatal blot on the landscape; their own parasitic presence is already a corruption of the traditional life of the people.

This is inevitable, because the beauty of the picturesque is a beauty created by a contrast between the spectator and his object. It is only because we feel ourselves the creatures of a sophisticated civilization that we enjoy the spectacle of a relatively unsophisticated life; if we lost that feeling, we should lose the pleasure which we now take in the picturesque. Hence we must, in order to sustain that pleasure, sustain in ourselves the feeling of separation from our object; we must live in the country without becoming countrymen, just as, in order to taste the peculiar pleasure of being on foreign soil, we must live abroad without becoming foreigners; or as, in order to feel the picturesqueness of a cathedral, we must visit it without being worshippers. To see anything as a thing of natural beauty, we must look upon it with consciously alien eyes; and therefore, when this object is a human society, we must resist absorption into this society and perpetually assert our alienation from it. This means the maintenance of a discordant note which, because its maintenance is essential to our own sense of the music's beauty, we do not feel as discordant: yet however blind the individual spectator may be to his own destructive influence upon the object which he is enjoying, he cannot be blind to the similar influence of others.

(c) But there is a third beauty which must be called a kind of natural beauty: the negation not of all human activity, nor yet of artificiality, but of the conscious intention to be beautiful. If artificiality means the departure from that bondage to natural conditions which characterizes a primitive society, an artificial civilization will necessarily destroy the beauty of primitive society even while it creates the enjoyment of that beauty; but yet its products have a beauty of their own which is not the beauty of art. The railway and the steamship and the factory are the negation of natural beauty in the senses in which we have hitherto discussed it, but they are beautiful, and their beauty is not, like that of a work of art, an intentional and designed beauty. They are meant to be useful, to carry out certain purposes as efficiently as possible; yet this very utilitarianism produces beauty at unawares, a beauty which, in its unconsciousness of itself, has the same essential character as that of a mountain or a field of wheat. Hence their beauty is dependent upon the singleness of aim with which their designer has bent himself upon the task of efficiency; power and speed, economy and strength, perfect adaptation of means to end, generate an austere grace and harmony which can only be disturbed by any conscious effort after decoration. An engineered road destroys the lines of a mountain as completely as a mill destroys the shape of a valley; yet the road's purposeful line and the mill's blockish building and pointing chimney have a beauty of their own, which may easily be spoilt by giving the road a rustic parapet and the mill a crenellated outline in a misguided attempt to embellish them. Such embellishment does not prevent the destruction of beauties to which, in any form, the road and the mill must be fatal; it merely prevents a new beauty from coming into existence. So the first motor-cars tried to save the beauty of the horse-drawn carriage, and only succeeded in being ridiculous; whereas the motor-car of to-day is only trying to be itself, and is therefore as beautiful as the *Aquitania* or the Lots Road power-station.

The subtle affinity between this form of beauty and that which was last described arises out of the principle that nature is only conquered by obeying her. The lines of a factory-chimney, a dam, a fast steamship, are so nicely adjusted to the natural forces which they are designed to counteract that they present to the eye visible graphs of these forces; as the curve and stoop of a sail make the wind visible, so these other lines make visible the weight of bricks, the thrust of standing water and the resistances of a disturbed liquid. Therefore these utilitarian devices for overcoming nature are infected with a tang of nature herself, and in so far as they are beautiful, their beauty is a reflection, perhaps a concentrated and intensified reflection, of nature's beauty. And this, again, is the reason why even in this third form natural beauty is a fragile thing, a thing to be enjoyed in silence for fear of breaking the charmed sleep on which it depends; because if the engineer is told that his works are beautiful, and reacts to the knowledge by aiming henceforth at beauty, employing architects and artists to collaborate in his designs, he will infallibly spoil hem. He will lapse into the Wardour Street of engineering, and end as a designer of steam yachts.

4 THE WORK OF ART

§ 17 *The Birth of Art*

The forms of natural beauty discussed in the last chapter make up a continuous line pointing in a definite direction. In the transition from the first form to the second, and from the second to the third, a principle is gradually emerging which, when it comes into the full light of day, puts an end to the privileged position of nature in the world of the aesthetic consciousness. This principle is that man can create beautiful objects; or rather, that his creativity is always and essentially a creation of beautiful objects. Human action, which at first appeared as a canker of ugliness distorting and defiling by degrees the face of the world, has been found capable not indeed of ceasing to destroy what is beautiful but of creating fresh beauties; first the beauty of a primitive society nestling against the bosom of nature, and then the beauty of a sophisticated civilization that has learnt to overcome nature by obeying her. But since the difference between a primitive and an advanced civilization is only one of degree, and every society regards itself as advanced and its predecessors as primitive, the cycle of the three forms is always complete at every point of the historical process; and therefore the principle of man's power to create beauty is always written large across human experience.

The recognition of this principle is the birth of art, in the narrower and stricter sense of the word. The designer of a power-station or a railway viaduct is an artist, but not a conscious artist: he is creating beauty, but not purposely. He becomes an artist in the strict sense by becoming a conscious artist.

When first we become conscious of our own activities we generally become less efficient in them; our self-consciousness upsets the instinctive balance and precision of our act, and we appear to have lost a faculty instead of improving it. A person who has never learnt to box or to sing or to practise farming, but has fought and sung and farmed as he picked up the art in everyday experience, is far more efficient than when first he begins to take lessons and tries to box or to sing or to farm scientifically. While he did not think about it, he did it reasonably well; when he starts thinking about it, everything goes wrong. But if we go on thinking, the first disastrous results of thought wear off; we not only form fresh habits, which become as spontaneous as those with which we began, and are developed to a higher pitch, but we also acquire the power to act in circumstances that lie outside our experience, and thus extend indefinitely the range of our faculty as well as intensifying its efficiency in any given field.

The transition from unconscious to conscious art is no exception to this rule. We become aware that we have been producing beautiful objects; for instance, beautiful gestures designed merely—so far as they were designed at all—to convey a meaning to our neighbors, or beautiful houses designed merely to keep out the wind and the rain. We then try to do the same thing consciously; and this first deliberate attempt at art seems to destroy natural beauty without creating anything else. Our gestures become awkward; our houses acquire an air of posturing and leering like the shapeless creatures of a nightmare. There is always something disheartening in such a change, and when we see it on a large scale we are apt to regard it as a sign that a whole civilization has lost its aesthetic faculty. But what appears as the morbid perversion of a taste hitherto pure is in reality nothing but the birth of art. Art, in the narrower sense of the word, the conscious pursuit of beauty, is here seen in the very act of emerging from the chrysalis of nature. This does not mean that the aesthetic consciousness emerges from something other than itself; that, for instance, a purely utilitarian society at a given moment achieves sufficient

wealth and leisure to devote some of its time to the enjoyment of beauty; for the aesthetic consciousness is the
absolutely primary and fundamental form of all consciousness, and all other forms emerge out of it. Nor does
it mean that there is any one historical period at which
the aesthetic consciousness passes over from the phase of
natural beauty to the phase of artistic beauty: to ask when
this happens, or happened, is like asking when a river
plunged over a waterfall. It is a transition which is always
going on and has always been going on, and is none the
less a real transition.

§ 18 *The Work of Art in its Immaturity*

The birth of art has already taken place when a child
covers a piece of paper with meaningless pencil scribbles.
These scribbles are not on the same footing as the child's
scream of anger or cry of joy, or the movements, often
very beautiful, by which it gives vent to its feelings and
energies. All these acts are below the line which divides
nature from art; they may be beautiful, but they are not
done because they are beautiful. They are the natural
foundation of art, beautiful to the spectator with the
beauty of nature, but precisely lacking that self-conscious
purpose which is absent in nature but present in art. A
child scribbles on paper not as an unreflective way of
giving vent to its energies but because it finds an aesthetic
pleasure in the scribble; the scribble is intended to be
beautiful, and is therefore at a higher level of activity
than the jump of joy. It is easy for the adult spectator to
overlook this, because the adult spectator sees beauty in
the jump of joy and none in the scribble, and therefore,
from his own point of view, prefers the former. And certainly the jump of joy is in itself a more finished product

than the scribble; yet it is only nature, whereas the scribble is art; and nature must reach maturity before she can conceive and bring forth even the feeblest infant art.[1]

The scribble is the work of art in its most rudimentary form; and the same form reappears in acts like swinging a leg or stamping a foot, beating a drum or blowing a tin trumpet, singing or whistling in a random and tuneless fashion, and countless other acts that may be noticed in all children and all adults. These acts are rudimentary works of art in so far as they are conscious sources of aesthetic pleasure; but on so low a level that they are often reprehended as fidgeting or suppressed as nuisances. Even the rhythmic movements of breathing or walking may become aesthetic acts by being tuned to a conscious rhythm, as in marching: a column of men on the march is an orchestra in which every instrument is a primitive drum.

But the work of art at this level is only a rudimentary work of art, because it is a random and uncontrolled production, enjoyed only so long as we do not care whether it is done well or ill. The scribbling child takes pleasure in his scribble just because it is a scribble, not because it is a good scribble; the note required of the tin trumpet is just any note, of any quality, any duration and any intensity; the drum is pleasant because it makes a bang, not because it makes one kind of bang rather than another. This undiscriminating joy in the production of anything whatever, not because it is this thing rather than that thing, but because it is simply, in the abstract, some-

1. A child may scribble not because it finds its scribble beautiful, but because it is pretending to be Daddy writing books or painting pictures. In that case the situation is complicated by an element of imitation, which will be discussed later. The case considered in the text is that of a child which is not consciously imitating any one or anything, but simply enjoying the act of making pencil lines on paper.

thing produced, is the bare minimum of art in the stricter sense: the beautiful is here anything which we ourselves produce, and the aesthetic enjoyment is the bare sense of our own creativeness.

This feeling is not only enhanced, but acquires a new quality, when by repeating such acts we learn to control them and modify them in definite ways. This control is the technical element in art. Technique is based on the realization by rudimentary art of its need for self-discipline, which depends on a growing dissatisfaction with bare creation and a desire to develop the power of creating this thing rather than that thing.

The acquisition of technique is what we call learning to draw, learning to sing, and so forth: and this means learning not how to make marks and noises, but how to make certain marks and certain noises. To be engaged on the task of acquiring technique in a deliberate and conscious manner is to be a student. The child who is not yet a student is unconsciously acquiring technique by merely going on scribbling; and the skilled artist has never finished perfecting his technique; but "study" in the special sense is an activity whose essence is concentration on the technical element in art, and the philosophy of the art-school is therefore the philosophy of technique.

Technique means, primarily, the muscular control which enables the creator to create exactly what he wants: draw the right line, sing the right note, and so forth. But secondarily, it is a training not of the muscles but of the eye and ear, or, more precisely, of the imagination, by which we become able to discriminate shades of form and sound which previously we had not observed to be distinct. Now this control can only be gained by the performance of set tasks. In order to check our ability to do exactly what we want, we must first know what exactly

it is that we want, and we must then be able to compare
this with what we have done. Otherwise, whatever line
we draw may be, by an easy self-deception, represented
as the very line we wanted to draw. Hence technique can
only be acquired by copying ready-made models, and
these models must be, not natural objects, but works of
art. The singing-master must sing a note for his pupil to
imitate, and tell him when he does it badly; the drawing
master must show his pupil how to draw by drawing. A
student is as likely to learn drawing by being set face to
face with nature as he is to learn Greek by being left
alone with a plain text of Homer. No doubt a very clever
student might, in such circumstances, find out how to
draw for himself; but the teacher's business is to supply
grammar and dictionary. Nor must the difference between the aim and nature of a student's drawing and a
master's sketch be forgotten. It cannot be too clearly
understood that a student's drawing is a technical exercise
and not a work of art. It has no business to be beautiful;
its business is to be accurate; and if it is called beautiful,
this is only because accuracy itself is aesthetically felt as a
peculiar kind of beauty. No art master would praise or
blame the work of his students on any ground but this,
and a student who takes the same liberties with his copy
that an artist takes with his subject is trying to run before
he can walk.

But the imitativeness of students' work is of value in
developing and strengthening the creative faculty precisely because it is not pure imitation but disguised creation. You can make a novice climb by roping him and
leading him; he supports himself because he thinks some
one else is supporting him. This applies to all education.
The student is really painting pictures of his own; his
own hand and eye are doing the work, and the copy is

only setting the pace. When the student awakes to the consciousness of this truth, he is no longer a student, but has graduated as a master.

§ 19 *Formal Art*

The child's scribble, after passing through the fire of technical training, emerges as a formal work of art, a skilfully-drawn scribble, that is, a pattern. So with the arts of song and gesture. The formal art of patterns, in whatever material, is the simplest type of mature and skilled art; for a pattern is a work of art in its greatest possible degree of simplicity, a work of art which owes nothing to any experience except itself.

But form is correlative to matter, and all artistic production, so far as it is formal, is the control and disposal of this or that material. There must be some material, for this material is at bottom nothing else than the nature which, as we have seen, is the presupposition of art: not the presupposition of the aesthetic activity in general, for that has no presuppositions, but the presupposition of the specific form of that activity which is art in the strict sense. Formal art, then, is the imposition of a specified form on a given matter, but this act is not the first appearance of beauty, for the matter is itself nothing but natural beauty, and that is why it can be raised to a higher power by the skill of the artist.

It is the essence of matter that it should consist of an endless plurality of distinctions. The patterns of formal art therefore embody themselves in materials whose variousness is of their very essence as materials; and this is the source of the plurality of the "arts," painting, music, poetry, sculpture, dancing, gardening, and so on *ad infinitum*. There must be an indefinite number of these, and it cannot be possible to arrange them in a logical scheme, precisely because they represent the indefinite plurality of matter as opposed to the organized unity of form.

But the material is not purely passive to the activity of the artist. Just because it has already its own natural beauty, it insists upon being handled in one way rather than another; and this recalcitrance, which is a handicap to a bad artist, becomes a positive source of inspiration to a good one. The artist studies his material and learns the "feel" of it: he defers to it and asks it for advice as to how best he may handle it. Nor is he left alone with his material; his work is always influenced by the traditions of design in which he has been brought up. Nothing in the whole history of art is more striking than the way in which, out of the infinite number of possible patterns, the artists of a certain period confine themselves to a tiny common stock which they modify very slowly and by very small changes. Thus tradition becomes a standard, and a special form like the fugue imposes itself upon a school in such a way that music comes to mean the fugue and musical beauty comes to mean conformity with the fugal standard. Hence we ask ourselves, concerning a given piece of design, not simply whether it is beautiful, but whether it observes the rules of its special form. Such a question is right and necessary, though it may easily become pedantic unless the critic realizes that the rules are not an external limit to the artist's work, but a presupposition which that work absorbs into itself; that in the actual life of an artistic tradition the rules are neither pedantically obeyed nor anarchically flouted, but reinterpreted and created afresh by each new member of the school in whose life the tradition lives.

The artist who has mastered the feel of his material

and the style of his school produces works which are no longer mere patterns, nor yet patterns crippled by the forces of material and tradition, but patterns deliberately based on and expressing these forces. A work of this kind cannot be understood or appreciated except by reference to the medium and the stylistic tradition. A marble statue, a violin sonata, or a Greek tragedy is the fruit of specialized training, and its beauty cannot be felt except by going through a specialized training. This does not imply that the artist or the spectator, in the actual moment of creation or enjoyment, is thinking about materials and rules. His experience of these things, as exemplified in other works of art, presents itself in this moment as a feeling colouring his aesthetic activity. The work of art remains a monad: the artist in creating it is aware of it only, and is not thinking of precedents, con-ventions, or earlier essays in the same material. But these things have actually conditioned his work; they are the stepping-stones by which he has reached this point of view; and they survive in the work of art, transmuted into the form of aesthetic experience. And it is precisely by having reflected on these things that the artist strengthens and develops this aesthetic experience. By knowing his own relation to his materials and tradition, by being the historian or critic of his own art, he becomes a competent artist, the master instead of the slave of his materials and tradition. Here, as at a previous stage (§ 14), reflection upon imagination colours imagination itself.

§ 20 Naturalistic Art

Naturalistic art is not an attempt to reproduce nature but an attempt to depict it. A painter does not try to repro-duce a mountain or a table, which would mean making another mountain or another table: an actor does not try to reproduce a murder, which would mean committing another murder. A mountain can be represented by a painter, and a murder by an actor, without any multiplication of geographical features or deaths. To depict an object is to produce, not another of its kind, but a work of art resembling it; depiction is the creation, in a different material, of a formal pattern suggested by the original object. Formal art is the creation of patterns suggested by the possibilities of the material and by other patterns in the same tradition: naturalistic art adds another source of suggestion, namely a natural object. Naturalistic art is thus formal art fertilized by natural beauty.

It might be thought that this additional source added nothing new to the aesthetic character of the work of art, because a suggestion is still a suggestion, whether it arises from art or from nature. But this would be a mistake. To create a work of art on the strength of a suggestion given by another work *in pari materia* is not only much easier than to do so on the strength of a suggestion given by a natural object—which is why the work of young artists is generally imitative, based on a knowledge of art rather than on a knowledge of nature—but it is easier because it differs in kind, it is a more elementary type of activity. Naturalism is a more advanced phase of artistic work than formalism. A "conventionalized" drawing of a natural object—the human figure, for example, reduced to geometrical terms—is not necessarily a degraded version of a "naturalistic" drawing. In general, the reverse is the case. A child begins drawing people in a purely "conventionalized" manner, and its drawings only become naturalistic as it learns to draw better. The transition from conventionalized to naturalistic representation of objects is an artistic advance; the transition from naturalistic to conventional, an artistic decline.

Naturalistic art is a modification of formal art; but this modification does not take place at a high level of development only. As there is a rudimentary type of formal art which is found at a very low level, so there is a rudimentary naturalism which is found wherever sufficient control has been acquired to permit its occurrence. As soon as a child has learnt to make one noise rather than another at will, it copies noises; for instance, a child eight months old, if it has a good ear, will imitate a motor-horn; and the proverbial imitativeness of children is due not to an "instinct" of imitation—such instincts are the *asylum ignorantiae* of bankrupt psychologies—but to the emergence of the naturalistic element in their imaginative life. Just as there is a constant overflow of aesthetic activity into outward expression, as we never enjoy any aesthetic experience without some play of gesture, a movement of the limbs, a smile or a frown, or the like, so there is a constant tendency for this outward expression to imitate the object in a material of our own: we gesticulate at a landscape, stamp our feet to music, and so forth.

Naturalistic art is an attempt to copy nature; but this is to attempt the impossible. Nature is so infinitely rich in detail, so infinitely subtle in her effects, that we cannot really copy her. The naturalistic artist is like a man writing a piano version of an orchestral score; he has to leave out practically everything, and misrepresent everything he puts in. And the harder we try to copy nature, the farther we get from her true spirit; because the meticulous elaboration of detail produces an effect of labour which is the precise opposite of the effortless fertility of natural detail. But if we cannot copy nature in her entirety, we must select; and selecting is idealizing, for the omission of some part of the object is not mere omission of a part but alteration of the whole. Naturalistic art is thus forced to idealize, consciously or unconsciously; and the only question is on what principle this idealizing is to be done. If nature is to be the artist's guide—an assumption essential to naturalistic art—nature must herself supply the principle. We must alter nature by reference to nature, which can only mean altering this particular instance of nature by reference to others. But what others? Every particular instance of nature is equally impossible to copy and therefore equally in need of idealization; and it follows that the criterion of idealization must be found in a purely ideal nature. What we are to depict, then, is a typical or generalized nature which is nowhere actual; and we alter the particular objects which we are ostensibly copying so as to bring them nearer to conformity with this norm or type. That artists actually do this will be questioned by no one who has any acquaintance with, for instance, the history of portrait-painting.

But the norm or ideal by reference to which we idealize nature is not actually found in nature at all. We may imagine it to be reached by an inductive study of individual objects, but this is simply an error. Nothing could be more palpably false than that a portrait-painter leaves out from the portrait of a lady every detail in which she differs from the other ladies he has seen. The ideal in question is an ideal of the imagination, created by itself for its own guidance; a law laid down wholly *a priori*, and independently of all experience of the natural world, by the pure act of the aesthetic spirit.

§ 21 *Imaginative Art*

At this point the naturalistic idea of art overthrows itself, and the discovery is made that naturalism rests on a principle of which it can give no account, namely the idealization of nature by a pure *a priori* act of imagination. The recognition of this truth brings us to the culminating phase of artistic creation, which for lack of a better name we may call imaginative art: the art in which the autonomy and self-sufficiency of imagination are vindicated and the naturalistic element is reabsorbed. A marble Aphrodite is at once a pattern in marble, because it stands or falls by the balance of its masses and the harmony of its lines, and a copy, because it reproduces the pattern which the artist found in a female figure. It idealizes that pattern, as any copy must; and so far, it does not differ from a naturalistic work of art. Where it differs is that it idealizes consciously. In carving a portrait-head the artist is idealizing, for he cannot help it, but he thinks he is copying; in carving an Aphrodite he knows that he is idealizing. By this knowledge he sets himself free from that servitude to idealization which we call mannerism. The portrait-painter has mannerisms which make him unconsciously alter the shape of an eye-socket, the profile of a nose, the position of a mouth; and these to some extent impair the perfection of every naturalistic work of art, regarded as naturalistic. But in the imaginative work of art they are no longer a handicap but an inspiration. As an artist masters his material by finding out what it can do, instead of trying to make it do what it cannot, so he masters his mannerisms not by eradicating them—for he would always develop others—but by converting them into merits, inventing imaginary figures in which these mannerisms, given free play, become beauties.

To say that the artist knows that he is idealizing does not mean that the actual work of aesthetic creation includes knowledge as part of itself. That is impossible; the work of art is always an act of imagination, not of thought. What is meant is that the act includes a feeling which, when analysed, reveals itself as an intuitive awareness of idealization: whereas the naturalistic artist does not experience this feeling, though analysis shows that he too is actually idealizing. Now when we feel a thing intuitively, this many mean that we have already explicitly known it, and it has come to colour our feelings; or that it is a mere feeling which has never reached the level of thought but is, as we sometimes say, "instinctive." Is it because the artist, as critic or historian of his own work, has become reflectively aware that he has been idealizing, or is it merely "instinctively," that the feeling arises in him which prompts him to desert naturalistic for imaginative art?

This question can be answered by considering the function of the title attached to a work of art. The title of a portrait implies that the artist not only is trying to copy something, but has reflected on his work and has explicitly discovered that he is trying to do so. The title of an imaginative work, for instance of a statue called Aphrodite, implies that the artist knows himself to have arrived at this aesthetic experience not by copying but by reimagining the beauty of the female figure and of a certain group of artistic works. Had he not reflectively known this, he might have carved the statue, but he would not have given it the name. The name implies a reference beyond the single aesthetic act; but the act itself has no such reference; the reference is therefore the work of reflective thought. The title of a work of art is an historical note explaining how the artist arrived at this point of view, and intended to help others to reach the same point. In so far as the statue is felt to need a title, the achievement of this monadic point of view is conditioned not merely by having passed through certain other experiences but by the artist's knowledge that he has done so.

The "subject" of a work of art is a similar reference from the work itself to the series of aesthetic experiences through which it was achieved. When people ask what a work of art "is about," they are trying to get an orientation or point of view from which to contemplate it. From its own point of view, the imaginative work of art is not "about" anything; it is only a naturalistic work of art that deliberately refers to a subject; but from the reflective point of view every work of art may be said to have a subject in so far as it is a resultant of certain experiences other than itself.

It may be asked at this point how imaginative art differs from formal art; for if the naturalistic element is reabsorbed, if the beauty of a statue depends wholly on the balance of its masses and the harmony of its lines, as was said at the beginning of this section, it might appear that the statue is after all a pure pattern and nothing but a pattern, in which case what has here been called imaginative art is nothing but formal art over again. In a sense this is true; the imaginative work of art does not appeal, in order to explain its own beauty or to excuse its own ugliness, to the naturalistic principle that the object depicted "was so," but feels itself perfectly free to depart from the object wherever this fails to satisfy its own imaginative standard of beauty. But none the less there is a perfectly definite distinction between formal and imaginative art, which may be seen by reflecting on their presuppositions. Formal art in its perfection presupposes that, first, the artist's materials, and secondly, the traditional rules of the form in which he works, have been so far mastered by his own efforts that they have become, as Beethoven said of the rules of music, his very obedient humble servants. Imaginative art presupposes this and also a further training, namely a training in naturalistic art. Naturalistic art in its whole extent is, from the point of view of imaginative art, a training, a process of discipline and education by which the artist absorbs the entire range of natural beauty into the materials of his work. And since, as has already been pointed out, the transition from formal to naturalistic art is a necessary transition, necessitated by the fundamental character of imagination itself, the return from naturalism to a new formalism in the shape of imaginative art is not only necessary in its turn, but gives rise to a new kind of art, which is not impelled to pass over into naturalistic art but has conquered that impulse by having gone through it and out to the other side, and is therefore its own master.

5   THE LIFE OF ART

§ 22   *The Work of Art and the Life of Art*

The creation of works of art is not the ultimate aim or crowning phase of the aesthetic life. It is a necessary phase of that life, and a phase which is never transcended, but one whose position in the life of art as a whole is quite secondary, and whose necessity is the necessity of a means rather than that of an end.

The question why a painter paints is not an unanswerable question, as it would be if painting were the real aim and end of the painter's activity. He paints in order to see. Until one has drawn it, one does not know what a thing is like; one has not observed it with that combination of attention to detail and attention to general effect which alone deserves the name of seeing. A person who does not draw has only a dim and vague feeling of the look of things, and at no single point has he a clear or accurate grasp of their appearance. As was observed in § 18, learning to draw means at bottom learning to see; and the whole of painting consists in an attempt on the the part of the painter to force upon himself a habit of precise observation. This progressive sharpening of vision is an infinite process; for as soon as the possibilities of precision in one direction seem likely to be exhausted, a different line of development suggests itself. Thus a painter who has done his utmost in observing detail may awake to the possibility of seeing relations between broad masses; in attending to colours he may have failed to notice the varying textures of things, and so forth. Similarly, the practice of music is a sharpening of our discrimination with regard to the pitch, intensity, quality and inter-relations of sounds; the drama and the novel perform the same function with regard to human nature. And in all these and like cases, the artist himself is intuitively aware of the instrumental character of his works. An artist does not want to build himself a picture-gallery in which to hang his own paintings, in order to enjoy their beauty. He prefers to stow them away in a lumber-room, or let other people look at them. To be compelled to look at them himself would be torment. The act of creation once over, the real product of this act is the continued and intensified activity, which has reached a new phase of its development by merely having passed through the old: and the artist now wants to begin painting another picture. The picture which he is about to paint is always going to be his masterpiece; that which he has lately finished is always a disheartening daub; those which he painted years ago are monuments of a distant youth upon which he looks back with mixed feelings, toleration and complacency, a little admiration and a little contempt.

The work of art is thus a phase in a dialectical process in which the aesthetic spirit by its own labour continually grows upon itself. As the ultimate standard by which the work of art is shaped is the pure art of imagination, so the life to whose advancement the work is an instrument is the pure life of imagination; for when an artist says that he paints in order to enable himself to see, this seeing is not the perceptual seeing of the common-sense consciousness, but simply imagination.

But the life of imagination is a life in which all human beings participate. Hence the work which the artist creates in order to advance his own aesthetic life is in principle capable of the same function in any one else's aesthetic life. In the act itself, this truth is not explicitly present. The artist does not paint for an audience, but for himself; and it is only by truly satisfying himself that he can truly satisfy others. But what he is trying to satisfy in himself is, whether he knows it or not, that imaginative activity which is the same in himself as in others; and it is no more possible that a work of art should be truly and ultimately beautiful to one person and not to others than that a scientific demonstration should be truly and ultimately cogent to one person and not to others. In both cases alike there are vast divergences between different people's requirements and satisfactions; but the principle at work in these divergences is the same in the two cases, and there is no more real difference of opinion as to the merits of Sophocles than of Aristotle, of Shakespeare than of Newton.

It is the implicit conviction of this truth that impels the artist to publish or exhibit his works, and to attach some importance to their reception. In making the work he has been trying to see something for himself; in publishing, he is trying to show the same thing to others.

§ 23 *Genius and Taste: The Classics*

The person to whom a work of art is exhibited, if it actually succeeds in conveying its point of view to him, has achieved a step forward in the dialectic of his own aesthetic life by its help. He therefore regards it as his master, as something from which he has learnt what he could not find out for himself. Between him and it there is the dialectical relation of patient to agent, a person who can follow and a person who can lead. This relation appears in every type of activity, art and science, religion and morals, economics and politics; and in art it takes the special form of the relation between taste and genius. Genius is the active or creative faculty, taste the passive or receptive; but they are not two faculties but two correlative phases of the single aesthetic activity, for the essence of genius is that it can lead taste, the essence of taste is that it can follow genius. Yet there is a real gulf between them, the eternal gulf between master and pupil, prophet and disciple, ruler and subject. The distinction is not one of degree; for though it is based upon a greater intensity of aesthetic activity on the one hand and a less on the other, it consists essentially not in this inequality iself, but in the recognition of the inequality and a deliberate adjustment of the inferior to his position.

The attitude of discipleship to certain artists erects

these into the position of "classics" or "masters" in the technical aesthetic sense. No one is a classic or a master in himself, but only in virtue of the habitual belief that we who call him so are permanently inferior to him in aesthetic power, and can take up towards him no attitude but that of learner or follower. To speak of the classics is to acquiesce in the conviction that one cannot create great works of art for oneself, though one has the taste to recognize them when one sees them; to claim for oneself at most the position of a minor artist whose achievements must always be immeasurably surpassed by those of one's masters.

This reverence for the work of others is a necessary phase in any healthy and progressive artistic life; a man must be a very bad artist indeed if he never, at any time of his life, thinks that Homer and Titian and Bach have done better work than anything he is likely to do. Yet there is a certain confusion in this attitude of unquestioning reverence towards the classics, and therefore a certain instability.

§ 24 *The Revolt against the Classics*

If taste were irrevocably inferior to genius, it could not even pay that respect to genius by which alone it is recognized as taste. A great man is great by thinking great thoughts; and if we cannot think his thoughts, we cannot know his greatness. But if we can think them, we raise ourselves to his level and become great also. This reflection cannot be dismissed by the argument that we think these thoughts only when we blindly accept what he tells us, and not by any power proper to ourselves; for if that were so, we should swallow everything that anybody told us with the same blind gratitude, and thus taste would be merely lack of discrimination, or lack of taste. To distinguish great from small we may indeed remain inferior to the great, but we must rise above the small; and then the only question is where to draw the line. Wherever we draw it, it must be a line to whose altitude we have flown on our own wings.

In short, only genius can understand genius. An inferior mind drags down the objects of its admiration to its own level. That aesthetic consciousness which labels itself as taste is really genius ignorant of its own nature; it thinks of itself as merely receptive and passive whereas it is in fact creative and active, creative of that standard by which it recognizes certain works as works of genius. In that recognition, the student of the classics thinks that their energy is, as if by magnetic induction, evoking a reflex of it in himself; but it is really his own creative imagination that discovers in their work a mirrored likeness of itself, for he finds in them just what he has in himself.

The advance in his aesthetic life which he had ascribed to the influence of the classics is therefore due simply to his own efforts to understand the classics; and when he discovers this he becomes conscious of his own freedom and power, and ceases to regard the classics as the source of his own activity. This discovery is the germ of that revolt against the classics which is a necessary and perpetually recurring phase of the life of art.[2] The genius, once sublime, becomes ridiculous, and the aesthetic spirit embarks on a campaign of iconoclasm against its own superstitions. It cannot simply ignore the masters whom it has worshipped, because its admiration for them has

2. It might be possible to claim for this permanent aesthetic category the name of Romanticism; but that word in actual usage seems to denote a certain historical period or event.

by its own act become ingrained and inveterate, and it is now bent on liberating itself from this servile attitude. It is fighting against itself, and fighting for its freedom; and the more in earnest it is, the more bitterly it must reject the authority which once it lovingly accepted. The fierceness of this revolt is due to nothing but the strengh of the hold which the once accepted master still retains on the loyalty of the rebel. The firmer is this hold, the more violent must be its removal; and hence the revolt against the classics is most intense and most painful precisely in those people who have best learnt what these classics can teach them, and have most keenly enjoyed the learning of it.

Some such revolt against authority, simply because it is authority, is a universal feature of all spiritual life. It is the counterpart and recoil of the opposite tendency to accept authority simply because it is authority: to obey simply because commands are given. In this blind obedience the spirit is free, for it obeys freely, but it is unaware of its own freedom; in the recoil from blind obedience to blind revolt it has become not only aware of it but obsessed by it and feverishly impatient of the lightest touch that reminds it of its former subjection. This movement from blind obedience to blind revolt underlies much of what recent psychology has fancifully called the Oedipus complex; and it is well symbolized by the story of the man who, when charged with beating his father, pleaded in defence that it ran in the family.

But in the mood of revolt the rebel does not realize that he is fighting against his own fixed habits. He thinks he is fighting against a definite and tangible enemy, Victorianism, the Eighteenth Century, Medieval Art, or whatever it may be. He falls into the optical illusion of thinking that all art has its merits except the art of the period immediately preceding his own, and the result of this illusion is always the same, namely that the rebellion against tradition or academicism rushes into the assertion of a new and equally tyrannous tradition, a new and equally narrow academicism. The rebel thus becomes in his turn a tyrant and an object of just hatred to other rebels. This cannot be otherwise, for rebellion is the destruction of what exists merely because it exists, and as soon as it has established itself it has become an existing principle, a system or dogma, and its own spirit is therefore logically committed to its destruction. Rebellion is in fact the purely negative side of all activity. An activity which does not lapse into stagnation must negate that which it is, in order to become that which as yet it is not; but negation by itself is simply nothing at all; it is annihilation, and therefore the rebel who was a mere rebel would be merely a suicide.

§ 25 *The Life of Art in its Freedom*

Rebellion is self-destructive, and burns itself out when it has destroyed that against which it is in revolt. The rebel is in revolt against himself, against his own spirit of servility; and therefore the spirit of servility and the spirit of rebellion expire together. Out of their death a new spirit is born, namely the spirit of freedom. The slave is free, but does not know it; the rebel is so much obsessed by the idea that he is free, that he cannot enjoy his freedom; but when we have ceased either blindly to follow our leaders or blindly to fight them, we can at last begin to walk beside them in a new-found friendship.

From this new point of view we can once more enjoy and admire great works of art; but this is a critical instead of an uncritical admiration. Not that we admire them the less for being critical of them; on the contrary, we admire them more, because great works become greater to an eye that looks at them through the clear air of candid appraisement instead of the smoke of idolatry.

This attitude may perhaps be described as the attitude of appreciation, the word being used in its proper sense and not as a mere synonym for admiration. To appreciate a work of art is to recognize its aesthetic qualities, to be sensible of its beauty. Every work of art has its beauty, and the attitude of appreciation is the attitude which approaches every work of art with the expectation of finding in it some beauty peculiar to itself. To achieve this attitude is to overcome all those prejudices which lead us to expect certain classes of work to be beautiful and certain other classes ugly; to approach certain things with a predisposition to find them beautiful because they are Greek, or medieval, or of the Ming dynasty, and other things with a predisposition to find them ugly because they are baroque or Victorian. Every period and school of art is aiming at something, at some peculiar type of effect which it feels to be worth achieving; and to be hostile to any given period or school means to deprive oneself of the aesthetic experience in which that period or school specialized, and so to impoverish one's aesthetic life to just that extent. To achieve this breadth of appreciation is not to be an historian or a critic; it is an aesthetic, not a reflective, activity. But it is the necessary basis for any sound historical or critical work.

The free life of art is this appreciative life, which is acquired by absorbing all that technical training can give, and through this training becoming increasingly sensitive to all beauty in nature and art. Such a life will necessarily produce works of art in its endless round of self-education, but these will be felt as mere points of emphasis or concentration in a process which goes on within the spirit itself; it will necessarily lose itself in admiration of nature and art, but only to recover its balance by finding in its own imagination an enhanced creativity. Its life will be nothing but the ceaseless flow of this creative energy, issuing eternally from its fountain-head in the pure act of imagination, and passing eternally through its cyclical phases, to end eternally as the pure act of imagination again.

To say this is not to describe an abstract or unattainable ideal, a metaphysical figment or a transcendent goal to-wards which the aesthetic spirit of man is struggling. It is to describe the actual facts which characterize the life of every artist. The life of art in its perfect freedom is that concrete life which every one, so far as he is an artist, enjoys. The unattainable, the illusory, is not this perfect freedom but those mutilated fragments of reality which a superficial analysis mistakes for reality itself: the sub-lime, the comic, formal art, naturalistic art, classical art, romantic art, and so forth. Yet every one of these is a real and distinguishable element in that pure act which is the free life of art.

6 *ART AND THE LIFE OF THE SPIRIT*

§ 26 *The Life of the Spirit: Art and Religion*

The life of the spirit is an indivisible whole within which are necessary and permanent distinctions: permanent in the sense that the spirit in its own activity perpetually re-affirms them, and necessary in the sense that the attempt not to affirm them would merely result in affirming them over again. Fundamentally, the spirit is awareness or consciousness, which implies a *prima facie* distinction between the conscious spirit and the world of which it is conscious; but since this awareness is itself an act, a self-modification on the part of the spirit, the passivity of pure awareness rests upon the creativity of action, and the life of the spirit is a whole within which consciousness and action, awareness of the world and modification of the world, are correlative elements. The unity of these two elements is feeling, where that of which we are aware is our own states, and these states are identical with the feeling of them: they are at once states of consciousness and objects of consciousness. Hence a rhythm in which awareness and activity concentrate themselves into the unity of feeling, and feeling again articulates itself into awareness and activity, is fundamental in all aspects of the spiritual life.

But life is not a mere rotation of three psychological categories in a rhythmical monotony. This triple rhythm is present in all life, but it is never twice alike; its whole character is altered by the specific differences of the experience in which it is embodied. These differences emerge in the course of a process which on its theoretical side may be called the spirit's attempt to know itself, on its practical side the spirit's attempt to create itself. To know itself means also knowing its world, and to create itself means creating its world; its world in the former case means the world of which it is aware, in the latter case the world in which it can live. There is a theoretical rhythm in the spirit's life, which consists of an alternate concentration on the external world and on its own nature, and a practical rhythm, which consists of an alternate adaptation of itself to the world and of the world to its own needs; and the unity of these two rhythms is an emotional rhythm consisting in the feeling of its unity with the world and its opposition to the world.

The first stage in this process is the life of art, which is the pure act of imagination. This is not only empirically the first stage observable in children and primitive peoples, it is necessarily the first stage. Awareness in itself, in its absolutely undifferentiated immediacy, can only be awareness of that which we immediately apprehend, and unawareness of that which we do not: that is, it is an act of consciousness which presents to itself an object of whose relation to other objects it takes no cognizance. As consciousness ranges over a field of objects, it illuminates that object upon which it falls and leaves all others in total darkness: the immediate object is its whole world and it knows nothing beyond. But this is that monadic consciousness which, as we have seen, is imagination; and all that has been done in the preceding chapters is to elaborate this concept of imagination and bring out enough of its implications to show its identity with what we ordinarily call the aesthetic experience. Action in itself, the undifferentiated immediacy of the practical life, consists in doing that which we do and nothing else; that is to say, immersing ourselves in an activity without any question as to the relation between this activity and anything else which at the moment we are not doing. To say this is to describe that form of action which we call play; and therefore play is the practical aspect of art, art the theoretical aspect of play. What characterizes each is its immediacy, that is to say, its concentration upon the activity of the moment and its ignoring of anything outside this activity. A game is what it is for no reason outside itself; is played as if there were nothing in the world but games, and no games but this game. Just as art does not explain itself by stating reasons, so play does not explain itself by stating reasons; and immediacy means the absence of reasons.

But this immediacy is not and cannot be a self-contained and complete form of consciousness. To imagine in a concentrated and truly imaginative way, one must know that one is imagining; and hence imagination rests upon its own opposite, thought. It is only within a consciousness which distinguishes truth from falsehood that we can find in actual existence that consciousness which does not distinguish them. Otherwise a cry of pain or joy would be the whole of poetry, a dream the whole of painting, an instinctive pursuit or flight the whole of dancing. The work of art is related to these things as the vertebrate to the amoeba; and the skeleton, unseen but indispensable, is thought.

The question "what am I?" can therefore no longer be answered in terms of imagination; I am not merely an imaginer but a thinker. The question "what is my world?" must be answered by saying that it is a world not merely of fancies but of realities. But if I who think am also the I who imagine, it would seem natural to superimpose the act of thinking on the act of imagining in such a way that the real is merely one division of the imaginary. The only world whose existence we have learned to recognize is the world of our own imaginations; and when the distinction between reality and unreality forces itself upon us, as it does the instant we come to reflect upon imagination, we impose this distinction upon the world of imaginations, and regard certain imaginations as true and others as false. To do this is to break with the life of art; for art knows nothing of the distinction, and merely imagines what it imagines and does not imagine what it does not imagine. But now we are asserting one imaginary object as real, and denying another as unreal; and to do this is to embark upon the life of religion.

It is a commonplace that all religion expresses itself in mythological or metaphorical terms; it says one thing and means another; it uses imagery to convey truth. But the crucial fact about religion is not that it is metaphor, but that it is unconscious metaphor. No one can express any thought without using metaphors, but this does not reduce all philosophy and science to religion, because the scientist knows that his metaphors are merely metaphors and that the truth is something other than the imagery by which it is expressed, whereas in religion the truth and the imagery are identified. To repeat the Creed as a religious act it is necessary not to add "All this I believe in a symbolical or figurative sense": to make that addition is to convert religion into philosophy.

Thus in religion that indifference to the distinction between real and unreal, which is the essence of art, is abolished. Religion is essentially a quest after truth and explicitly conscious of itself as such a quest. But the truth which it can and does discover is a truth which is always hidden from view in a reliquary of symbolism: we see the imagery, but we do not see the truth; we are only conscious that the truth is there, and its presence converts the beauty of the imagery into holiness. But inasmuch as this holiness is a property of a mere symbol, religion always contains an element of idolatry and superstition.

§ 27 *Science, History, Philosophy*

Religion consists of a perpetual attempt to overcome its own initial error, to destroy superstition and idolatry, to reach the spirit behind the letter. But success in this attempt is the death of religion; when the metaphor becomes conscious metaphor, when the thought is distinguished from the imagery in which it has been wrapped up, the symbol loses its holiness and becomes merely significant. Language and thought now fall apart, and language becomes the mere instrument of thought. In art the presence of thought— for we saw that thought was present—was wholly forgotten, and the object of attention was pure language, or rather an imagery which, because not explicitly correlative to thought, was not yet explicitly language; in religion thought was immediately identified with the language expressing it, and was therefore never truly expressed. But with the achievement of that distinction between letter and spirit which is the goal of religion, we have reached the life of explicit or self-conscious thought.

To separate thought from language, intellect from imagination, and to concentrate on thought as distinct from imagination, is the characteristic of that type of consciousness which we call scientific. Here thought is regarded as an activity self-contained and self-sufficient, and its object as a self-contained and self-sufficient intelligible world, reached through, but lying behind, the sensible world. The aim of science is to apprehend this purely intelligible world as a thing in itself, an object which is what it is independently of all thinking, and thus antithetical to the sensible world, which is admittedly relative to our apprehension of it, being in fact nothing else than the world of imagination which is at once the object and the creature of the imaginative activity. The world of thought is the universal, the timeless and spaceless, the absolutely necessary, whereas the world of sense is the contingent, the changing and moving appearance which somehow indicates or symbolizes it.

But this very separation of reality from appearance, the necessary from the contingent, creates a problem which to the scientific consciousness is insoluble. The appearance must somehow be an appearance of the reality; the contingent must somehow be grounded in the necessary. Appearance and reality, imagination and thought, have been merely distinguished and not related: they must somehow be brought together again and shown to be equally necessary, each to the other. This need is satisfied by the historical consciousness, whose object is the individual; no longer an abstract universal divorced from its own equally abstract particulars, but a universal that particularizes itself, a particular constituted by its own universality. For history, the truth is no longer an abstract necessity which nowhere actually exists; it is concrete and actual, it is real in every sense of the word, while the truth of science is a reality which is in one sense utterly unreal, an ideal never realized, a law which has no instances.

Even in history, however, there is a relic of the abstractness of science. This relic consists in the separation of subject and object. The fact which is the object of historical thought is a thing in itself, a thing whose existence and nature are supposed to be wholly independent of the thinker; the task of the thinker is to discover a world of fact which is "already there" for him to discover. And hence there is still in history a failure to realize the unity of thought and action. The historian is a mere spectator, he does not modify the world but apprehends it. He is a man of thought, a student, not a man of action; and however strongly he feels his kinship with the men of action whose actions he studies, he only feels it and does not actualize it.

This abstractness is only overcome in philosophy. The

object of philosophy is nothing short of reality, a reality which includes both the fact of which the historian is aware and his awareness of that fact. The philosopher is the thinker who not only thinks but knows that he thinks and makes it his business to discover the implications of this. He is not, like the historian, outside his own picture; he sees himself as part of the historical process which he studies, and therefore part of his problem is to understand how that historical process has thrown up in its development an organ—namely himself—which is at once a part of it and the spectator of it. With this clue in his hand, rooted in the fact that he is both the child and the spectator of the historical process, he is able to reinterpret that process itself, and to see in every phase of it a nisus towards self-consciousness. And in realizing that history is the emergence of the spirit's consciousness of itself he is actually achieving that consciousness, and bringing into existence, in his own person, that awareness of itself which he finds to be the fundamental characteristic of spirit. His knowledge is therefore explicitly action; he is creating himself by knowing himself, and so creating for himself an intelligible world, the world of spirit in general.

§ 28 *The Unity of the Spiritual Life*

The five phases of spiritual life which we have enumerated in this crude outline—and other phases which further analysis might distinguish—are not species of any common genus. They are activities each of which presupposes and includes within itself those that logically precede it; thus religion is inclusively art, science inclusively religion and therefore art, and so on. And on the other hand each is in a sense all that follow it; for

instance, in possessing religion we already possess philosophy of a sort, but we possess it only in the form in
which it is present in, and indeed constitutes, religion.
The unity of the spiritual life is a unity of the same kind
as the unity which we have already seen exemplified in
the life of art. Art as a whole, we saw, is the pure act of
imagination, and this act has its life in a process of self-
differentiation and self-concentration, diastole and sys-
tole, which generates the various forms and phases of
aesthetic activity within the unity of imagination itself,
and having generated them treats them as so much material by the mastery of which it vindicates this unity.
The act does not find a material, given from without, to
unify which is the problem of its life; it generates the
material out of itself and thus sets itself the problems
which it lives by solving. In the same way the life of the
spirit differentiates itself into art, religion, and the rest
in order that it may exhibit its own unity in this diversity;
or rather, that it may through this diversity bring into
existence a unity which is not the bare unity with which
it began but a unity enriched by all the differentiations
through which it has passed. This process takes place in
time, but it is an eternal process: it is always beginning,
it has always reached any given point, and it has always
arrived at its conclusion, somewhat as—to revert to a
previous simile—a river is always rising at its source,
always flowing over each part of its course, and always
discharging itself into the sea. But because the process
of the spirit is a conscious process, like a river which
should be aware of itself throughout its course, it does not
merely travel through a fixed cycle of changes, but finds
every passage past a given point altered in significance
by the consciousness of what has gone before it; and hence
the unity of the spiritual life resembles the unity of an

infinitely increasing spiral rather than the unity of a rotating circle. The energy which causes the spiral to expand is simply that pure activity which is the spirit.

§ 29 *The Mortality and Immortality of Art*

The spirit is pure act; the aesthetic spirit is the pure act of imagination. But to speak of the pure act of imagination is a contradiction in terms, for the qualification implies a distinction between imagination and thought, and an activity from which another activity is distinguished is by definition not a pure activity but one limited by, because correlative to, another. There is therefore no such thing as this life of pure imagination which is the life of art. Art is not a life but a subordinate element or phase in a life which is indissolubly one, the unitary life of the spirit.

Hence art always has its centre of gravity outside itself. It is not a self-contained and self-sufficient activity, but a mere segment of that trajectory which is the spiritual life as a whole. The aesthetic spirit, which from its own point of view is the pure negation of self-transcendence, is seen from the reflective point of view to have its very being in its self-transcendence, its passage from the life of art to another and a fuller life, from the monadic world of imagination to the world of reality whose essence is its transcendence of all monadism. This has always been seen by those who have regarded art as a means of education, an activity especially proper to children because a natural propaedeutic to the intellectual life of maturity; and some such view of art has been universally held by the greatest philosophers, both ancient and modern. But such a view would be misleading if it were taken to mean that art is nothing but a toy to be left behind in the nursery. There are two ways in which the peculiar value of art and beauty may be vindicated, and their claim to an essential place among the possessions of the human spirit defended: first, by insisting upon the aesthetic activity as it is in itself, by pointing out that beauty merely as beauty is an irreplaceable and infinitely precious possession, insufficient perhaps to fill the whole of life but yet admitting of no substitute that can even begin to console us for its loss; and secondly, by pointing out that in the aesthetic activity we achieve a symbolic or imaginative vision of the universe, the premonition of a truth to be reached in its explicitness by science and philosophy. We may value art for what it says, because what it says is beautiful; or for what it means, because what it means, but does not say, is true.

Neither vindication of the worth of art is true to the exclusion of the other. Beauty in itself, as an immediate and self-contained value, is certainly a thing without which the world would be poorer, a thing which nothing else can replace; but that does not prove that we ought, on this or that given occasion or indeed ever, to pursue it when there is truth to pursue. We are still exposed to Plato's reluctant conclusion that art is an eye which must be plucked out if we are to enter the kingdom of heaven. On the other hand, to regard beauty as nothing but a confused vision of truth is to take the heart out of it, to treat the aesthetic experience as a necessary evil, a stage in the road towards truth which is valueless in itself and desirable only for its ultimate consequences. One view makes beauty a form of vice, the other a form of physic.

But though no "apology for poetry" can be based on either point of view taken separately, the convergence of the two gives us a conception of art for which no apology is needed. Art is the immediacy of experience; and though there can be no immediacy without implicit mediation, neither can there be mediation except as resting on and penetrated by immediacy. Imagination is not thought, and unless thought is present there can be no imagination: yet imagination is the focus, the luminous centre, of all thought. The attempt at a self-contained life of art is therefore of necessity futile. An art which hugs itself in the conviction of its own self-sufficiency and pretends to exist for its own sake is an illusion, and can only end by becoming invertebrate and unproductive. But as art actually exists, it exists not in this isolation, but in the closest union with thought; what has by thought been grasped becomes expressive, because immediate, in the form of art, and thus every achievement of every other phase of the spiritual life passes into art, there to be focused into a luminous point from which it can reissue into the explicitness of thought.

Thus art in itself is a phase of consciousness which is always being transcended; its instability involves it in a death which takes place not at a certain moment of development in the individual or the race, but at every moment. But in its relation to the spiritual life as a whole, art is immortal, and at every moment it is created anew in the shape of the immediate consciousness which the spirit has of itself, the ever-springing fountainhead of the spiritual life.

§ 30 *Art and its History*

The particular forms which art assumes at any given period of human history are necessarily mortal. None of

them is or can be a joy for ever. Not only are the individual poems and paintings of individual artists doomed
to a merely material corruption, but they must become
objects first of hatred and then of indifference to the
world that has accepted them; its very enthusiasm for
their beauty generates a revolt against themselves and
the ideal for which they stand. It is no more possible for
an individual work of art to be thought beautiful for
ever, than for an individual man to live for ever. But they
await a resurrection, and some do not await it in vain.
A time may come when people shall rediscover the beauty
of this work, done by artists long dead, and value it not
merely archaeologically but aesthetically. This interest
in the art of distant ages is such a familiar thing in the
modern world that we are apt to regard it as normal, and
to forget that it is a thing of comparatively recent origin
and comparatively small extent. It did not exist at all in
the greatest period of the ancient world. The Greeks
cared nothing for the art of their Minoan predecessors, or
for the beauties of Egyptian sculpture. The Romans admired Greek work, but they regarded the Greeks rather
as contemporaries, carrying on the tradition of the old
masters, than as representing an age wholly removed
from their own. It was not till that reverence for an-
tiquity, which so strongly marked the spiritual life of the
Middle Ages, had culminated in the Renaissance, that
the modern faculty of admiring ancient art established
itself. And even now this faculty is the fruit of special
education, and only exists in a very small minority of
people. Contemporary art is the only art whose appeal is
direct and spontaneous; and that is because it embodies
imaginatively the experience of the contemporary world.
We are all, though many of us are snobbish enough to

wish to deny it, in far closer sympathy with the art of the music-hall and the picture-palace than with Chaucer and Cimabue, or even Shakespeare and Titian. By an effort of historical sympathy we can cast our minds back into the art of a remote past or an alien present, and enjoy the carvings of cavemen and Japanese colour-prints; but the possibility of this effort is bound up with that development of historical thought which is the greatest achievement of our civilization in the last two centuries, and it is utterly impossible to people in whom this development has not taken place. The natural and primary aesthetic attitude is to enjoy contemporary art, to despise and dislike the art of the recent past, and wholly to ignore everything else.

But this resurrection of ancient art, effected by the growth of our modern historical consciousness, is not a revival of the past. That is impossible. We may read Chaucer with enjoyment, but we cannot be Chaucer; our experience is not his experience, and therefore our imaginative outlook is not his. We see in Chaucer's poems something that he did not see there, and do not see what he saw there. And in many cases it is perfectly certain that the qualities which we admire in ancient works of art are the opposite of the qualities which their contemporaries enjoyed. A work whose greatness in its own day consisted in its paradoxical audacity is enjoyed to-day for its innocent conventionality by people who detest audacity and paradox; and it is a typical irony that we should admire Greek statues for their whiteness.

What is true of individual works is true of styles and forms. Painting nowadays means painting easel-pictures; but this is a recent innovation in the history of art, and not one that is likely to endure. The ballad, the play, the symphony, and all such forms, depend upon historical circumstances which cannot be permanent. The work of art itself is on a different level. What new forms it may take in the future, no one can pretend to know; we can only be certain that they will not be those which it has assumed in the past.

But the transformations which art undergoes in the course of its history are the expression not of a self-contained life of art which initiates its own new forms by a dialectic of its own, but of the life of the spirit as a whole. Art, as art, has no history. Art means the aesthetic activity, imagination: and imagination is the act of presenting to oneself a complete, self-contained, monadic world which exists only in and for that act. Every such act ignores every other; From the aesthetic point of view for which alone art exists as art, nothing exists except one individual work of art at any individual moment. From the historical point of view the work of art does not as such exist; all that exists is the imaginative act, and this imaginative act is seen as a resultant or expression of activities which are not imaginative. Hence there is no history of art; there is only the history of humanity. The force which transforms art from one shape to another as this history proceeds is not art, it is that force which reveals itself in history as a whole, the force of the spirit. Hence no event in the so-called history of art can be explained by reference to the principles of art itself. To explain the history of architecture, we must study the technique of building construction and the social purposes which buildings are intended to serve; to explain the history of music, we must study those forms of social organization which give rise to choirs and orchestras; to explain the history of painting, we must begin by asking what people have painted with, and upon what they have painted, and why. And no history of literature can begin to be history in the true sense of the word unless it is a history of religion, of science, of philosophy, and of ethical and political ideals.

What is commonly known as the history of art, just because it neglects these principles, is not history at all. It is a mere chronicle of facts whose connexion with each other is merely temporal and spatial. The task of history is to show why things happened, to show how one thing led to another. But one work of art does not lead to another; each is a closed monad, and from one monad to another there is no historical transition. Our ordinary histories of art are magic-lantern shows in which we are invited to contemplate first one work of art, and then another, and then another; as if an historian should think that he had discharged his whole duty when he had told us that this year there was an earthquake, next year a battle, and the year after that a famine.

The same is true of criticism. What is usually called criticism is the mere expression of opinion upon the aesthetic qualities of works of art; it is in fact what in § 25 has been called appreciation. The true function of the art-critic is not simply to say that he likes this and dislikes that, but to explain works of art; that is to say, to put people, including himself, in possession of information which will enable them to appreciate intelligently. Now a work of art as such cannot be explained; it is self-explanatory or nothing. What can be explained is the process by which the artist reached this particular point of view. As has already been pointed out (§ 21) the title given to a work of art is an indication of this process, and is intended to enable others to repeat the process and so reach the point of view at which the work of art explains itself; and the function of the critic is to do this on an extended scale. Hence the history and criticism of art are the same thing: namely the history of the human spirit in general, regarded as an activity of thought which, transcending the monadism of art, makes the advance of the aesthetic consciousness at once possible and intelligible.

Suggestions for Further Study

It is impossible to become even tolerably competent in the philosophy of art without two qualifications: a training in art and a training in philosophy. (*a*) Every one enjoys to some extent the beauty of natural objects and works of art, and expresses his enjoyment in acts which are themselves works of art: but this does not entitle him to lay down the law about art. He must first develop and discipline his aesthetic powers by working long and seriously at the technical problems of some medium which should be that of music, painting, or the like, rather than the too familiar and therefore less instructive medium of words. Looking at pictures and listening to music are inadequate for this purpose: the student must learn to draw and compose. Without this artistic training, the philosophy of art must perish for lack of matter; the philosopher is trying to reflect without having anything to reflect upon. This is an extremely common fault in the books written about art by philosophers and psychologists. The notion that it can be mended by psychological observation of other people's experiences is a childish blunder. (*b*) On the other hand, books written by people whose artistic experience is profound often fail through lack of training in philosophical thought. This training can only be acquired by general philosophical study, not by study of the philosophy of art taken by itself: a philosopher of art who is not competent in all branches of philosophy is necessarily incompetent in the philosophy of art. Our educational system makes it difficult for the same person to receive both these trainings: but not impossible.

Subject to these warnings, the following books may be mentioned as especially deserving the student's attention. The first group consists of introductory works, critical and historical.

1. CARRITT, *The Theory of Beauty* (Methuen, 5s., second edition). This is the best general introduction to the subject in English, and consists chiefly of critical discussions of the most important theories.

2. BOSANQUET, *History of Aesthetic*: or,

3. CROCE, *History of Aesthetic*, being Part II of his *Aesthetic* (English translation, second edition, Macmillan, 1922. The second edition alone is complete and trustworthy).

The second group comprises the chief landmarks in the history of thought on the subject.

4. PLATO, *Republic*, especially books II, III, X (translation Jowett).

5. ARISTOTLE, *Poetics: see* S. H. BUTCHER, *Aristotle's Theory of Poetry and Fine Art.*

6. VICO: *see* CROCE, *Giambattista Vico* (English translation).

7. KANT, *Critique of the Judgment* (English translation).

8. HEGEL, *Aesthetic*: the whole work translated by F. B. P. Osmaston (four volumes), the *Introduction* alone, with an introductory essay by the translator, by B. Bosanquet. A highly-compressed statement of Hegel's view as to the place of art in life in his *Encyclopaedia,* §§ 556–553 (= WALLACE, *Hegel's Philosophy of Mind,* pp. 169–74).

9. CROCE, *Aesthetic* (see above). A more compact and mature statement of the view is in his *Breviario di Estetica*, translated under the title *The Essence of Aesthetics* in the volume *New Essays on Aesthetics.*

It is impossible here to say anything of the vast mass of books on art written by artists; but such books are nearly always worth reading, though the views which they express are, as a rule, one-sided and exaggerated.

Plato's Philosophy of Art

I T HAS been usual in recent years to regard Plato's account of art, in the tenth book of the *Republic*, not as a theory of art but as an attack on art; an attack based on a misunderstanding of its nature so complete and so unwarranted as to defy explanation, except on the hypothesis that Plato was either speaking ironically or influenced by motives which ought not to weigh with a philosopher. Something like a general agreement seems to exist among editors of Plato and writers of treatises on aesthetic, to the effect that Plato has, in this passage at least, wholly failed to grasp the nature of art, and that we should look in vain to this passage for any serious contribution to the science of aesthetic: for the whole passage, we are told, rests on the blunder of regarding the work of art as a reduplication of perceptible objects, whose value, so far as it has a value, is therefore the same in kind as the value of the objects which it reduplicates. This accusation has been so repeated and developed by

Reprinted from *Mind: A Quarterly Review of Psychology and Philosophy*, XXXIV, N.S. (1925), 154-172.

one writer after another that to rebut it might seem hopeless; yet the aim of this paper is to maintain that Plato never for a moment exposes himself to it, and that the blunder lies wholly on the side of his interpreters.

For this purpose I shall begin by giving a short abstract of the passage in question (595-608), and then try to state what exactly is the view that Plato is here expounding; after which I shall briefly consider certain important passages in other works where the same subject is again treated. I do not wish to suggest that everything maintained, whether by Socrates or by any other character, in a Platonic dialogue is necessarily the view held by Plato himself; and at the outset I shall treat the thesis maintained in the *Republic* merely at its face value, as a position held by a character in a dramatic work. But the comparison of this position with relevant passages in other works will, as I hope to show, strongly suggest that the view here expressed by Socrates is Plato's own.

The passage opens with the formal statement of a thesis to be defended: namely that poetry (ποίησις) is an intellectual danger to everyone who is unprovided with an antidote in the shape of a knowledge of its real nature. On this it may be observed (1) that though poetry is the immediate theme of the discussion, the phrase περὶ ποιήσεως being the title of the λόγος, the sequel shows that Plato is fully aware of the substantial identity of nature which unites poetry with painting: (2) that though Plato no doubt regarded his own myths as works of art, μῦθοι as opposed to λόγοι, there is here no condemnation of the use of such myths, in so far as the mythologising philosopher understands the nature of the weapon he is using.

The thesis is now developed and defended as follows:—

1. *The Doctrine of the Three Degrees of Reality.*

Three orders or grades of objects are distinguished: first, the absolute and eternal form, wholly real and wholly intelligible: secondly, the perceptible object, copied from the form: and thirdly, the work of art, copied from the object. The form of a bed is an object of the first order, the perceptible bed made by a carpenter is an object of the second order, the picture of a bed made by a painter is an object of the third order. It is important not to confuse objects of one order with those of another; for, if we mistake those of the third order for those of the second, we fall into the mistake of supposing the artist to be skilled in all those crafts which make the objects which he depicts—the error of imagining that the epic poet understands strategy and politics, and so forth. This error, the error of supposing that the artist makes nature when in fact he only holds the mirror up to nature, arises through failing to understand that the work of art stands on a wholly different plane, belongs to a different order of being, from the objects made by the craftsman.

2. *The Doctrine of the Three Degrees of Knowledge.* This is a consequence of (1). The value of an object of the first degree is absolute and unconditioned. The value (ἀρετή, κάλλος, ὀρθότης) of one of the second degree is not absolute, but relative to the need (χρεία) which it satisfies: hence its maker, as such, does not know why it should be made in one way rather than in another, but has to assume that the user knows what he wants, and obey orders. *A fortiori*, the value of an object of the third degree is not absolute, but is relative to the corresponding object of the second degree: therefore the artist's grasp of this value, which, like any other apprehension of an object, must be conditioned in character by the object apprehended, is a third order of knowledge related to the second as the second to the first. Now the second, the crafts-

man's knowledge, is strictly not knowledge but opinion, an opinion guided by someone's knowledge, an opinion about knowledge; and therefore the artist's knowledge is opinion guided by someone's opinion, an opinion about opinion; opinion of the second degree.

3. *The Doctrine of the Emotionality of Art.* This is a development of (2), just as (2) is a development of (1). Knowledge can justify itself by appeal to demonstration; opinion cannot demonstrate itself, but it can appeal to authority; art, as opinion about opinion, can do neither, and therefore its standard can only be the standard of immediate feeling. Our perceptions, says Socrates,—perception being quoted as an instance of opinion—are liable to error, but we can correct this error by measuring, counting and weighing, thus appealing to something other than perception to test the correctness of perception, as the bridle-maker appeals to the rider to settle the question whether his bridles are well made. The object of the second degree refers directly to an object of the first degree, and this enables us to disentangle the right opinion from the wrong. But in the case of objects of the third degree there is no such reference, and therefore no possibility of distinguishing truth from error. This distinction has, at the level of art, simply disappeared; and art therefore lies at the vanishing-point of reason. But since human nature is compounded of reason and emotion, the vanishing-point of reason coincides with the absolute rule of emotion. Art encourages and appeals to emotion as such; its ruling principle is the passions, which in a happy and well-ordered life must be controlled by reason; and hence the aesthetic experience is a psychological anarchy, an orgy of misrule.

The passage ends with an epilogue, commenting upon the argument from a personal point of view. The peculiar danger of art, says Socrates, lies in the fact that it appeals most strongly to the best men; and this is why we cannot neglect the problem, but must in our ideal state admit only that poetry in which this dangerous weapon of emotional appeal is wisely used. And if this seems severe, we are only too anxious to hear anything that can be said in mitigation of its severity; for obviously such ardent lovers of poetry as ourselves can only stand to gain by any relaxation in its favour, so long as we do not forget that our first duty and interest is to keep before ourselves the ideal of the best life. If it is asked why Socrates permits certain forms of art to be retained in the ideal state instead of consistently banishing all alike, the answer is surely obvious: these are, in the opinion of Socrates, the forms which art will take in the hands of men who understand its true nature.

The key to the whole passage is the conception of imitation or copying (μίμησις). The current misinterpretations of the passage are based on assuming that when Socrates speaks of copying he means that kind of activity by which a carpenter makes a chair resembling another chair, or an artist paints a picture resembling another picture. Now this is precisely what is not here meant by copying. A copy, as the word is used in this passage, means not a facsimile or replica, that is, an object of the same order and possessing as far as possible the same characteristics as the original, but an object of a wholly different order, having the characteristics proper to that order, but related by way of resemblance to an object of another order, and having in that resemblance the ground of its peculiar value. Thus, the carpenter copies the form of a bed. He does not, in doing so, produce a second form of a bed; Socrates is careful to point out that he cannot; it is the essence of a form, that it cannot be reduplicated. What

the carpenter produces is not a concept or intelligible object, an object of the first order, but a percept or visible
object, an object of the second order; and a percept whose
value consists in its relation to the form of a bed, its attempt to embody that form in perceptible shape. This
perceptible bed is not related to the form as its instance,
for it is not an instance of "bedhood"; it is not an embodiment of the universal bedhood, but only an attempt at
such an embodiment, a more or less unsuccessful attempt. This is because the perceptible as such is tainted
with imperfection, unreality, unintelligibility: hence the
attempt to embody the perfection of the concept in perceptible shape is a self-contradictory attempt, and fore-
doomed to failure. The perceptible bed is not an instance
of bedhood, but only an approximation to bedhood; and
it is this idea of approximation that Socrates expresses by
the term copying. To copy is to construct in a given
material an object resembling one which is not made in
that material; and the material itself imposes an impass-
able restriction on the fidelity of the resemblance. This
conception has an obvious reference to the artist's attempt to represent in a given material, as well as that
material will allow, an object in a different material.

> ἡ δὲ μελαίνετ᾽ ὄπισθεν, ἀρηρομέῃ δὲ ἐῴκει
> χρυσείη περ ἐοῦσα· τὸ δὴ περὶ θαῦμα τέτυκτο.
> (*Iliad*, Σ. 548-549) .

But in the *Republic* the merely empirical gulf which
separates the gold of Achilles' shield from the earth of the
ploughed furrows has widened into a metaphysical gulf
between appearance and reality, appearance being conceived as an imitation of reality, a copy of the conceptual
world in terms of perceptible objects. It may, no doubt,
be argued that the notion of copying or imitation is in-

adequate to bear all the weight that this doctrine puts upon it; but, for the moment, we are concerned only to see what the doctrine is.

The definition of art given in the *Republic* is that in art this same process is repeated at a further stage. As the percept copies the concept, so the work of art copies the percept. This does not mean that the work of art is a facsimile of a perceptible object, possessing the same characteristics and claiming the same kind of value; it means the precise opposite. It means that, just as the percept is on a wholly different metaphysical plane from the concept which it copies, so the work of art is on a different plane from the percept; it possesses none of the characteristic attributes of percepts, but has attributes altogether peculiar to itself. Yet in so far as it has a value, this value depends on its relation to the world of percepts, just as the value of a percept depends on its relation to the world of concepts. As the perceptible bed is judged by its relation to the ideal of bedhood, so the picture of a bed is judged by its relation to the perceptible bed.

It is sometimes objected that in point of fact the artist is not limited by his model; that in the best art, at least, the artist depicts the model not as it is but as it ought to be; and that this is actually recognised in the *Republic* itself, where it is pointed out (472 D) that a painter may paint a man more beautiful than any man actually existing; and the moral is drawn that the artist really copies not the percept but the concept, not the actual but the ideal. But this objection is simply a confusion of thought. To copy the concept of man would be to make a man, in other words to live an actual human life. The painter, whatever he paints, paints pictures and nothing but pictures; and any picture is judged as a picture by reference not to the ideal of humanity, the concept of man in general, but to some particular man, whether this particular man actually exists or not. To suggest that the artist copies the form or concept is to suggest that the landscape painter, in painting a cottage, alters it so as to bring it into the closest attainable conformity with the concept of an ideal residence, and that the dramatist, so far as he is a good dramatist, depicts his characters as purged of all moral imperfections and regulated by the standard of what a man ought to be. These suggestions are of course absurd; the concept, the ideal which the craftsman would realise if he could, is a thing of which the artist knows nothing. What the artist produces is not a bed or a battle or a hero or a villain, but an object *sui generis,* to be judged not by the standards by which these things are judged, but by a standard peculiar to itself. That is the negative side of the conception of art as double imitation; and it is hardly necessary to add that it is the very foundation-stone of all sound aesthetic theory. To distinguish art from science and morality and handicraft and to assert that it has a sphere of its own; to distinguish the value of its works from scientific truth and from practical utility, and to place them in a distinct metaphysical category; this is the first step towards any real philosophy of art.

But there is more than this merely negative implication in the doctrine of the three degrees of reality. There is also implied a positive account of the relation between each degree and the next. The world of perception is wholly distinct from the world of thought, but not merely distinct. It has a positive relation to it, which is expressed by saying that it copies it. Similarly, the work of art, though wholly distinct from the world of perception, has a positive relation of the same kind to it. This cannot mean that Socrates is expounding a crudely naturalistic view of art as a quasi-photographic reproduction of nature; anyone who makes that suggestion need only be invited to explain how nature can be a quasi-photographic reproduction of a world of concepts; and this, if anything can, will convince him that it is dangerous to jump at what may seem the most obvious interpretation of the term μίμησις. Certainly Socrates maintains that art copies nature; but we have not yet explained what he means by copying; we have only explained what he does not mean.

The answer is to be sought in the *Republic* itself. In the sixth and seventh books Socrates elaborately expounds a conception according to which the universe is stratified, as it were, into various grades of reality.[1] Only the highest grade is absolutely real, and ultimately therefore the other grades do not exist at all; they are appearance, not reality, but they actually do appear, and therefore from the point of view of human life it is necessary to give an account of them. Now to say that only the highest grade is real, is to say that it alone is absolutely possessed of its own attributes; is unreservedly what it is; is such that a true account of it is possible. Elsewhere we find things, or ostensible things, which are not what they are; things possessed of contradictory attributes, that is not really possessed of any at all; things of which—not through the fault of mind or language, but by reason of their own inherent unintelligibility—no account whatever can be given. Or rather, an account of sorts can be given of them, but it will be a self-contradictory account; it will ascribe to them contradictory predicates, and these

1. In the interpretation of this passage and the making use of it to explain the account of art in the tenth book, I have been greatly helped by Mr. H. J. Paton's paper on *Plato's Theory of* εἰκασία, in *Proc. Arist. Soc.*, xxii. (1922).

predicates will be terms having a genuine applicability to the real and to nothing else. This grade of things or quasi-things which are approximately describable in terms of reality is the grade next below the highest. So far as it is anything, it is a confused or perverted version of the highest grade; and so far as we can understand or apprehend it at all, we can do so only by thinking of it as such a confused version of the real. But this relation which subsists between a reality and a confused version of it is capable of reappearing at a further stage, in the form of a relation between the confused version of reality and a confused version of this confusion. This third grade, the perversion of perversion, will again be approximately describable in a sense, but only approximately describable, in terms of the second grade, that is to say in terms of what is itself a confusion; and hence the third grade is unintelligible in the second degree. Further, in such a series of grades it is shown at the end of the sixth book that each grade will develop within itself distinctions of a similar kind to those which separate it from the others; thus each will show the same general type of structure with each other and with the whole. The study of this structure, which enables the philosopher to pass out of the lower grades into the region of reality, is called dialectic.

This theory of grades of reality is indisputably the key to the *Republic* as a whole and, in particular, to the conception of imitation. Each grade imitates the one above it; that is, tries to be what the one above it is. Now this, translated out of the terminology of the object into that of the subject, means that there are as many forms or grades of experience as there are grades of objects, and that each grade of experience involves the error of believing that one is enjoying the next above it; or rather, simply is that error. For the inferior grades are, by definition, not real; that is to say, the *real* universe is not stratified into these grades but is wholly contained in the highest grade. The other grades are only appearance; they are in fact reality itself as misconceived by persons labouring under various types of error. Hence it is not really correct to speak of degrees of reality, as if there really were a distinction between objects more real and less real, which is of course absurd: the distinction is in point of fact only a distinction between degrees, or rather powers, of error. Hence the term μίμησις expresses not the resemblance between two real things, nor even the relation of a less real thing to a more real thing; it expresses the relation between an appearance and the reality which it appears to be. This is seen in the case of the bed; the perceptible bed is called a copy of the form precisely because it is not a bed at all, but something which we call by the name bed because we fall into the error of thinking that the ideal of bedhood has been embodied in it, when in fact it has not. The source and ground of the distinction between the grades is sheer error. Remove error, and the system of grades disappears.

Art copies nature, then, in the sense that aesthetic experience is concerned with an appearance of an appearance. The world of perception is not real; it is only appearance; and the world of art is not this appearance itself in its actuality but an appearance of it only. Art is not knowledge, for it cannot be praised for its truth, and its object is not the concept. It is not opinion, for it cannot be praised for its utility, and its object is not the percept. It is not, like knowledge, the apprehension of necessary truth; it is not, like opinion, the forming of judgments which may, with luck, be true. It has no concern with truth at all, either essentially or accidentally. The

object of art neither is real nor appears to be real: in
other words, the aesthetic experience neither is nor believes itself to be knowledge. What, then, is the right
name for it and for its objects? Its own right name is
imagination, and that of its objects is phantasms or
images (φαντάσματα, εἴδωλα), sheer appearances apprehended and indeed created—if that can be said to be
apprehended and created which does not exist at all, but
only appears—by an activity resembling, if not identical
with, dreaming. This imaginative activity does not assert
anything; hence the artist lacks, not only knowledge, but
even (602) opinion; and his works contain no truths, nor
even assertions which by some chance might be true, but
only a glamour which when stripped off leaves nothing
behind (601). This glamour is what we call beauty; and
here again one can only say that the view propounded by
Socrates is unquestionably sound aesthetics. True, the
"glamour" is not called κάλλος; but κάλλος does not mean
beauty. It means goodness or rightness or utility; the
quality of serviceableness in a thing like a bridle; it is
explicitly equivalent to ὀρθότης and opposed to πονηρία. As
the Greeks have no word for art, so they have no word for
beauty: but it would hardly be true to say that on this
account their philosophers did not to some extent grasp
the conceptions to which we apply those names. We have
seen that Plato realises at least the substantial identity of
painting and poetry; and when he wishes to speak of
beauty he uses such words as ἡδονή, κηλεῖσθαι, ἔρως; and no
one accustomed to Plato's use of terms will be surprised at
this or argue that these words commit him to what we
should call a hedonistic theory of beauty.

The "glamour" of art, beauty, is for Socrates an essentially emotional thing, and art is in consequence an
exercise of the emotions, not an exercise of reason. This

doctrine of the emotionality of art is liable to misinterpretation. Croce, who is far too sound a critic to fall into the main error which it is the object of this paper to criticise, has tripped here: for he remarks (*Estetica*, ed. 4, p. 185) that Plato, while rightly denying that art is concerned with the concept, failed to discover any theoretical activity except intellect, and therefore reached the false conclusion that art was nothing except sense and emotion. But no one has more emphatically than Plato, or at any rate the Platonic Socrates, maintained the existence of opinion and imagination side by side with intellect. This is the whole burden of the long and elaborate discussions of the grades of reality and of knowledge to which we have already referred. The emotionality of art, as Socrates conceives it, is a deduction from its imaginative nature. If each grade of objects is what it is by trying to embody an ideal drawn from the next higher grade, if each is a μίμησις of the next above, imagination is what it is by being a μίμησις, at two removes, of truth. The first remove substitutes for the demonstrability of truth the certitude of perception; the second remove substitutes for this the glamour or emotional atmosphere which clings to the phantasm. If we ask why the phantasm possesses this glamour, the answer is: because the phantasm indirectly symbolises truth. Symbolism, by its very nature, is the apprehension of truth veiled or disguised in an imaginative form; and truth so disguised is felt rather than thought: that is, it is present to the mind in the form of an emotional atmosphere clinging to the symbol. The symbol is heavy with an import which can only convey itself in the shape of a feeling of urgency, a feeling that there is something here which is of supreme value, a feeling that we are in the presence of a mystery revealed and yet not revealed. This is why art makes the peculiarly strong emotional appeal which, as Socrates points out, it does make to thoughtful and intelligent people; and this is why the struggle against its appeal, which Socrates so vividly describes, has its peculiar bitterness. If the emotionality of art were a merely sensuous reaction, the struggle against it, the old quarrel between poetry and philosophy, would be merely another case of the irksome but not heartrending warfare which all must wage against their animal lusts. The struggle against art is the struggle to resist the emotional appeal of a symbol in order to penetrate to that which it symbolises. And unless we are content to acquiesce in a merely negative theory of the relation between imagination and thought, a theory which exhausts itself in the assertion that they are different things and that there is an end of it, we must attempt to find between them at least some such positive relation as that which Socrates is here defining. The view of art as symbolic of philosophical truth has in the past been pushed by hasty interpretation to the point of obvious absurdity; and it appeared to be altogether a gain when such interpretations were simply swept aside by the assertion that art is imagination and nothing more, that its value is a value which it possesses altogether in its own right and in no sense borrows from anything else. But the real value of such an assertion lies in its provisional isolation of a problem which in the nature of the case cannot be finally understood in isolation. Sooner or later we must raise the question whether mind is not a genuine unity, in spite of its differences.

The view stated by Socrates, at any rate, is that mind is such a unity, and that its various grades of experience are linked together by a progressive dialectic. Art is one grade, but not the highest; it is essentially a primitive form of experience, existing at a level anterior to the distinction between truth and falsehood. From this doctrine emerge two final conclusions. First, because art is symbolic of activities other than itself, it is a preparation for these activities. In the life of art the immature mind enjoys a simulacrum of the life of explicit reason, a life which it is not yet able to enjoy except through such a mirror. It is not truth or morality or utility, but it prepares the mind for a direct acquaintance with these things; and therefore beauty is the mother of truth and goodness, and art is the corner-stone of all sound education. This is the doctrine of the early books of the *Republic*. Secondly, because art is not truth and morality but only symbolic of them, it is not an activity which ought to distract the attention of mature and educated men from direct contact with the realities which it symbolises. This is the burden of the polemic against the life of art in the tenth book. These two doctrines, so far from being contradictory, are complementary.

But we must not overstate Socrates' polemic. The specialised and isolated form of aesthetic experience which we call *par excellence* the life of art is certainly by him excluded from the ideal state, as being no true element in the life of reason; but aesthetic experience as such remains for him a permanent and necessary part of the life of reason, in so far as that experience is modified or controlled by reason itself. As we have seen, art is not banished from the ideal state. It remains the great educative power by which the young guardians are to be trained; and even the mature guardians are to continue in the practice of it, in shapes suitable to their intellectual and moral stature.

Such is the general view of art stated by the Platonic

Socrates in the *Republic*. We have now to consider certain passages in other Platonic dialogues bearing on the same subject.

1. In the *Apology* (22 A-C) Socrates is made to expound certain observations about poets; and these observations have remarkable points of resemblance with, and difference from, the view stated in the *Republic*. Socrates here threats the poets and the craftsmen separately, attributing to them quite different mental characterisics; this already shows in germ the distinction between the arts and the crafts. Further, he claims to have discovered that poets do not work by σοφία, but φύσει τινὶ καὶ ἐνθουσιάζοντες: that they do not understand their own sayings, and that their poetical gift does not mark them out as "wiser" in general than other men. Here we have unmistakably the negative side of the *Republic* doctrine; art is not knowledge, and therefore on the principles of Socrates himself not morality either. But this discovery is presented as a matter of mere experience; it is not brought into contact with any philosophical theory of mind in general, far less deduced from such a theory. Nor is there any attempt to state anything at all corresponding to the positive side of the *Republic* doctrine, the characterisation of art as an imitation and of its objects as phantasms. Of course this does not prove that Socrates, or Plato when he wrote the *Apology*, had not arrived at such a doctrine; the *Apology* would in no case have given a suitable opportunity for expounding it. What it does prove is that the negative side of the *Republic* doctrine had actually been formulated either by Socrates, or at least by Plato in this his earliest period of writing. And since there is much to be said for the view that Plato's *Apology* represents with substantial accuracy the speech that Socrates made, we may

accept it as a reasonable working hypothesis that Plato owed at least the negative side of the *Republic* theory to Socrates himself.

2. The *Ion* is generally regarded as a somewhat early work, though it is too short to be subjected with confidence to the tests of stylometric chronology. I here assume that it is earlier than the *Republic*: a closer dating of it is not required for the present purpose. It is *prima facie* a criticism not of the poet but of his interpreter the rhapsode; but in the course of the dialogue Socrates lays down very clearly certain views on poetry itself. Poetry is a divine power, like that of the magnet (533 D), and the artist's effects are due not to skilful craftsmanship but to inspiration (533 E); a musician composes in a Bacchic revel, feeding on honey-dew and drinking the milk of paradise, and not in an act of thought (534 A); hence the poet is an airy being, a sacred bird whose song depends on his banishing from himself all thought and reason (534 B). The thesis here maintained is identical with that of the *Apology* and the negative side of that in the *Republic*: namely that art is not knowledge, but actually requires the absence of knowledge, and also that it is not craft or skill. If we ask what it is, there is here no answer; to call it a divine force or an inspiration is simply to call it a *je ne sais quoi*. The doctrine of the *Ion* is purely negative, and is developed in detail by showing that Homer, the poet whom Ion's profession compels us to discuss, cannot be justly praised as a source of useful knowledge, although Ion takes the view that he can (536 E, *seqq.*). This topic is dealt with again and more fully in the *Republic* (599-600); and Ion's attitude shows quite clearly that the position there maintained was regarded by professional literary men as heretical. The passage in the *Republic* becomes more intelligible when we bear in mind

that Socrates is here attacking a utilitarian view of art which was generally accepted by contemporary opinion.

3. The *Symposium*, with its eloquent discussion of beauty, has often been regarded as the *locus classicus* for a view of art at once more appreciative and more true than the polemics of the *Republic*. But this opinion seems to rest on a misunderstanding. We have seen that κάλλος is not necessarily what we call beauty; and in the *Symposium* it is surely clear that τὸ καλόν is not the beautiful in the sense of the object of aesthetic contemplation, but the object of desire; the desirable or good. The traditional sub-title ἡ περὶ ἀγαθοῦ is perfectly correct: the word καλόν is here the name of that οὗ πάντ' ἐφίεται. So powerful is the current illusion of aesthetic theory in the *Symposium*, that a distinguished writer on Plato has twisted the remark about ποίησις in 205 B into a statement of the creative power of art, whereas the context shows it to be a mere observation as to the literal meaning of ποιεῖν, efficient causation.

4. Chronology now brings us to the *Republic*; and here for the first time we find a doctrine of what art is. Moreover, we find this doctrine not in the third book but only in the chronologically later tenth. Why is this? It will be argued by those who hold the Platonic Socrates to be identical with the historical Socrates, that throughout his literary career Plato had known the theory which he ascribes to Socrates in the tenth book, but that he had never before had occasion to state it. But this position, though *ex hypothesi* incapable of direct refutation, involves difficulties. First, there is no single hint, in any earlier work, of the positive theory now first enunciated, whereas we shall see that in later works it is uniformly assumed as both true and familiar. Secondly, the earlier works hitherto quoted actually betray the lack of such a

theory, by positively describing the poet's work in terms which amount to a mere *asylum ignorantiae*. It is not true that the Socrates of the *Ion* has no occasion for a positive statement of the nature of art; he clearly tries to give such a statement, and fails. This is very curious if, when he wrote the *Ion*, Plato already possessed the theory stated in the *Republic*. It becomes more than curious if we compare the *Ion* with the *Phaedrus*, to which we shall come before long. Thirdly, there is a remarkable change of terminology within the *Republic* itself. In the third book some art is mimetic and some is not; and the principle to be followed in education is that of using non-mimetic art freely and mimetic art only under certain restrictions (392 D—396). In the tenth book the subject is introduced by saying "we were right to disallow art ὅση μιμητική" (595 A) and going on, in defiance of this still implied distinction between mimetic and non-mimetic art, to argue that all art is mimetic and that this is in fact the key to its whole nature. Nor does Plato ever again in later works assert or imply the existence of non-mimetic art. This is, I submit, unintelligible except on the hypothesis that Plato arrived at the theory of art as double imitation after writing the third book of the *Republic*. On these grounds I shall hereinafter proceed on the hypothesis that the positive side of Plato's theory is his own, though he probably owed the negative side to Socrates.

5. In the *Phaedrus* the negative doctrine of the *Apology* and *Ion* reappears, explicitly supplemented by the positive additions made to it in the *Republic*. We learn not only that poetry is enthusiasm or inspiration, divine madness as opposed to the sanity of reason (245 A, with much even verbal resemblance to the speech in the *Ion*), but that on this account the poet comes low in the scale of souls (248 D, where the sharp distinction between

the φιλόκαλος and the poet is noteworthy), and that literary art, which is a game (cf. Rep. 602 B, παιδία τις καὶ οὐ σπουδή), may be a noble game (παγκάλην παιδίαν, with the usual non-aesthetic sense of καλός) if it devotes itself to telling stories (μυθολογεῖν) about things just, noble (καλῶν) and good (276 C-E); but that this noble game is surpassed by the still nobler work (σπουδή) of dialectic (276 E). The illustration in this passage, drawn from the comparison of gardening with playing at gardens, shows past doubting that Plato has in mind the notion of art as μίμησις and of its products as εἰκόνες of another order of things, and the correlative notion of art as a propaedeutic to philosophy, a game which is the undeveloped soul's introduction to work. In the *Phaedrus*, therefore, a positive view of art is pre-supposed, very different from the vague language about enthusiasm which it still, though with a deepened meaning, employs; and this positive view is precisely that of the tenth book of the *Republic*. Plato is here not re-opening the question of the nature of art; he is rather assuming that the result of the discussion in the *Republic* are to stand, and building upon them in order to discuss the relation between philosophy and rhetoric.

6. The treatment of art in the *Laws* is of special histor-ical importance. Whatever may be the case in other dia-logues, there is no reason to think that here Plato is expressing any views other than those he actually held at the time of writing; and therefore, when we find, main-tained or presupposed in the *Laws*, a view which has been dramatically expounded in an earlier dialogue, we have some reason for saying that even in the earlier dialogue it represented Plato's own position, whether or not it also represents a position held by the person in whose name it is there set forth.

The discussion of art in the *Laws* expresses or presup-

poses a theory of its nature in complete agreement with
that whose growth we have traced in the earlier works.
The second book discusses the place of song and dance
in the education of the young, and explicitly recognises
their necessity throughout human life; though it is assumed that their true value in adult life is that of a
recreation or relaxation from work, and that this recreation must be so organised as to bring it into harmony
with the fundamental aims of adult life. Throughout this
book it is maintained that songs and dances are mimetic:
εἰκαστική τε καὶ μιμητική (668 A), εἰκόνες (669 B) and, more
explicitly, μιμήματα τρόπων (655 D). Hence, Plato argues,
their value can be properly judged only by one conversant with the reality which they copy, the substance of
which they are the shadow (τὴν οὐσίαν, 668 A; the doctrine
of two removes is not explicitly stated, but appears to be
presupposed rather than abandoned). This is the reason
why we must not allow poetry to be controlled by the
judgment of a popular vote (658-659). All this is the
doctrine of the *Republic* both on its positive and on its
negative side. Later, in the seventh book, the question of
dramatic performances is raised. Both tragedy and
comedy are to be admitted, the latter because learning to
ridicule the contemptible is a necessary part of learning
to admire the admirable; but comedy is to be played only
by slaves and foreigners (816 D). When our city is visited
by tragic actors, we shall say to them, "we too are actors,
for our whole city is designed as an imitation of the no-
blest and best life" (this is an obvious reference to the
doctrine of double imitation). "But for this very reason
we shall not allow you a free hand; we shall submit your
plays to a strict censorship, and subsidise those we approve and ban those which we do not" (817 B-E). There
is nothing here inconsistent with the principles laid down

in the *Republic*; on the contrary, the views maintained in the earlier work are used as premises from which the details of the later are developed. True, the *Laws* permit drama, whereas the *Republic* permits no kind of literary art except hymns to the gods and praises of good men (*Rep.*, 607 A); but this is a difference not of principles but of their interpretation. Granted that the best and most rational life will admit into itself only an art controlled by reason, it still remains an open question what this art will include; and the dramatic censorship of the *Laws* is perhaps a better means of achieving the end aimed at than the restrictions as to subject and form which are prescribed in the *Republic*.

Thus, throughout his literary career, we find Plato consistently maintaining that art is something quite distinct from knowledge, morality and utility, something *sui generis*: and that its object is therefore not the real or the good or the useful, the object of knowledge or opinion, but an object as unique as the act of apprehending it. This view he may have owed to Socrates. In the tenth Book of the *Republic* he supplements this by a positive theory of what art is: it is imagination, whose object is an image or phantasm, and whose emotional character derives from the fact that this phantasm is not the real but a symbol of the real. This positive theory, we have seen reason to believe, was a discovery of Plato's, made between the writing of the third book of the *Republic* and the writing of the tenth. When first he stated it, he felt it to be beset by difficulties and advanced it with some hesitation (607-608); but later thought only confirmed it and all his subsequent references to the subject assume it as sound.

Plato's philosophy of art would perhaps have proved less perplexing to modern readers had it been expressed with less heat. It can hardly be doubted that the subject is one on which Plato felt strongly, and the strength of his feelings has powerfully affected his language; notably in the tenth book of the *Republic*. It is impossible to refrain from asking what it is that Plato felt so strongly when he wrote this passage. Readers sometimes fancy that what he felt was the puritanical moralist's objection to art as such; that he is writing as a fervent and bigoted partisan of the respectable as against the beautiful. But this is to forget that Plato is, after all, an artist of the first rank, one of the world's greatest masters of prose style and dramatic form. Now a man does not attain this rank as an artist without taking trouble, and one must be a very bad critic of literature if one cannot see that Plato cared intensely about the purely artistic side of his work. Whatever accusations can be brought against him, no one can accuse him of being a Philistine. Others, again, have imagined that Plato attacks art in general because the art of his time was decadent. But was it? That it was, is freely alleged by people complacently ignorant of the history of ancient art; yet Plato's own prose bears the stamp of decadence no more than do the carvings of Scopas. And if it was, did Plato think it was? No one has produced any evidence that he did. On the contrary, he habitually illustrates the faults of art by quoting Homer. And if it had been decadent, are Plato's criticisms thereby accounted for? Not at all. On the contrary, it would show the grossest ineptitude in him that he should pick a quarrel with art as a whole on metaphysical grounds when he really only wanted to quarrel with contemporary art on aesthetic grounds.

It may be worth while to suggest another explanation of Plato's heat. He was at once an artist and a philosopher; and in his early works the artist seems to predominate. His first writings have the appearance of being dramatic sketches written by a man with a strong interest in philosophy, but an even stronger interest in the drama of philosophical discussion. They are literary essays rather than philosophical essays. Now it is notorious that the later works of Plato show a progressive absorption in philosophy, a progressive alienation from the literary form of the mime. It is possible that this change did not take place without an effort. It is possible that Plato felt within himself a real conflict between the claims of his literary genius and those of his philosophical; and that it became gradually clear to him that he could only enter upon the kingdom of philosophy by deserting the field of pure literature. The consciousness of this conflict first becomes apparent in the *Symposium*, and it is this that gives to that dialogue its peculiar emotional tension; the same tension, gradually relaxed as the battle decides itself in favour of philosophy, is present with diminishing force in the *Phaedo, Republic* and *Phaedrus*. The world to which the philosopher must die is the world of art, the world of intuitive semblance or imagination. This is by no means the explicit doctrine of the *Phaedo*, but it is, unless I am mistaken, the ultimate meaning: and in the allegory of the Cave it becomes all but explicit. It emerges into full daylight in the tenth book of the *Republic*, where art and philosophy reveal themselves as parties to an "ancient quarrel," rivals for the supreme allegiance of mankind; and the violence with which Plato here rejects the claims of art is surely proportionate to the hold which he feels art to possess over his own mind. The "ancient quarrel between philosophy and poetry" is to be sought not in the earlier history of Greek thought, where its traces are, to say the most, meagre, but in Plato's own life; and possibly also in the life of Socrates, sculptor by

training and philosopher by choice. This conflict between two powerful tendencies in Plato's mind becomes a
matter of more than biographical interest if it is true, as
Plato himself believed, that a similar conflict must of
necessity arise in the mind of everyone who participates,
as every human being must participate, in these two
universal activities. From this point of view it becomes
clear that Plato can at once, without inconsistency, em-
phasise the value and importance of art and denounce it
as if it were a deadly sin. If to say that art is a permanent
and necessary element in human life is to praise it, then
no one has praised art more emphatically than Plato; if to
say that it is not the only and not the highest element
is to revile it, then no one has more emphatically reviled
it. But those self-constituted champions of art who rush
in to protect it against Plato's calumnies are easily answered in words of his own: ἀλλ' οὗτος μὲν ἐάν ποτε γνῷ οἷόν
ἐστι τὸ κακῶς λέγειν, παύσεται χαλεπαίνων· νῦν δὲ ἀγνοεῖ.

Yet there is a sense in which Plato does underestimate
the value of art: not that he misunderstands the true place
of art in the life of mind, but that he misunderstands the
place of mind in the universe. Reality is, for Plato, not
subject but substance; not mind but something which
may or may not become the object of mind's contemplation. We human beings, if we are to know reality, can
only come to know it through a course of educative experience which necessarily includes art as one of its
phases, though an early phase; but if we do come to know
reality, our knowledge of it makes no difference to reality
itself. The real world does not demand, as a condition of
its own being, our knowledge of it; there is included in
the nature of things no reason why this same nature of
things should ever become an object of knowledge. But
if there is no reason why there should be such a thing as

knowledge, there is no reason why there should be such a thing as art; for the only reason why art is valuable is that it forms an indispensable element in that human life whose highest function is to know reality. If our knowledge of reality in no way enriches reality itself, *a fortiori* our art in no way enriches reality. If the worth of human life is to be judged by its relation to a reality wholly other than itself, then knowledge has by this standard a certain worth, because in knowledge we apprehend such a reality; but in art we do not, and therefore art has no such worth at all.

This is a consequence following necessarily from Plato's "realistic" view of the relation between mind and its object. If the object is wholly independent of mind's knowing it, it follows that knowledge itself, and therefore everything presupposed by knowledge, is a mere contingent fact without a reason in the nature of things. Intelligibility, according to this doctrine, is to be sought not in intelligence itself but in the independent object of intelligence. Intelligence itself is unintelligible, and the stages in its development are doubly unintelligible. If there is no theory of knowledge, but only a theory of the thing known, *a fortiori* there can be no theory of art; and because art is not knowledge and has not a real object but only an imaginary object, there cannot even be a theory of its object. A realist can only avoid this conclusion by committing himself to a radical falsehood about the entire nature of art, and maintaining that art is not imagination but a kind of knowledge, whose specific object, the beautiful, is a specific element in the real world. If Plato avoided that error, it was because he knew too much about art.

But if intelligence itself is intelligible, if in philosophical thought the mind itself is its own object, then whatever is involved in the act of knowing is to that extent intelligible. And if the act of imagining is an essential phase of the activity of coming to know, as Plato rightly thought, then the aesthetic consciousness is no mere contingent, irrational or unintelligible fact, but a possible object of philosophical thought, a constituent element of reality.

The Place of Art in Education

No subject excites more general interest at the moment than education; and if a certain vagueness and inconclusiveness seem to infect most discussions about it, that is only because the subject has so many aspects—psychological, financial, administrative, and so forth—that one aspect is apt to obtrude itself before another has been sufficiently considered. In the hope of forwarding the general discussion, and in the belief that so large a territory can only be conquered by dividing it, I propose to raise a single question: What is the place which art occupies, or ought to occupy, in a system of education?

Occupies or ought to occupy, I said, as if the terms were synonymous. And so, in a sense, they are. For so far as art has not, in any particular educational system, the place which rightfully belongs to it in education as such, so far that system forfeits the title of education. And since people have contrived at all times and in all places to get education of a sort, those features, whatever they may be, which necessarily go to make up education must needs

Reprinted from *The Hibbert Journal*, xxiv (1926), 434-448.

exist in all places and at every time. To that extent education, like everything else, always is what it ought to be;
and even the most fanatical reformer, who only wants to
shatter the existing world in pieces that he may remould
it nearer to his heart's desire, might do well to bear in
mind that it could not be remoulded nearer to the heart's
desire were it not already within measurable distance of
it; were it not already, in some sense, a recognizable embodiment of its proper ideal.

We are concerned, then, both with education as it is
and with education as it ought to be, both with the actual
and with the ideal; both with the place already taken by
art in educational systems and with the place which it
would take in a system better than those which now exist.
This reflection is important because we are apt to miscon-
ceive, in our endeavours at reforming things, the relation
between the ideal and the actual; and it is important to
realise that art can have no place whatever in an ideal
system of education unless it already has a place in all
actual systems. The ideal is not attained by adding to the
actual what it does not possess, but by confirming its hold
upon its own essential nature—by showing the actual
how it can truly obey those laws whose binding force it already feels. Neither education, nor politics, nor religion,
nor anything else, can be improved by introducing into it
what are vulgarly known as "stunts"; but only by a more
penetrating vision of its proper and fundamental nature
and a more sustained effort to realise this nature in everyday life. And everything I shall say in this essay, however
abstract and philosophical it may seem to be, will be said
with the single object of improving the actual practice of
teaching, by improving, so far as in me lies, the teacher's
conception of what teaching is.

With the art school, the vocational training of the

specialised artist, I am not concerned. There must be specialised artists, and there must therefore be a special vocational training for them, as for all specialists; but the problem here to be considered is the place of art, if it has a place, in an education designed not to make artists better artists, but to make men and women better men and women; a universal education, universal not in its application—not, that is, to be uniformly imposed upon every single human being—but in its aim; an education directed to the betterment of human nature in its universality.

When I say that the purpose of education is the betterment of human nature, I mean that the purpose of education is to make the pupil fitter for life and better able to deal with its problems than he would have been without it. Education is essentially forward-looking or preparatory; its function is to prepare the pupil for something that lies beyond itself—for what, by antithesis with education or the school, we call real life or the world. And whereas a vocational training is a preparation for a specialised calling, universal education, or education in general, is a preparation for life in general. There is, perhaps, a danger that the necessity of such a general education, as distinct from vocational training, may be overlooked or denied under the stress of our economic scramble for existence; but its necessity is in general recognised by people with a clearness directly proportional to their experience of educational work and the thought they have given to the subject; and I shall not here undertake its defence.

In what sense, then, if in any, is art a necessary element in the preparation of life in general? The answer will evidently depend on what we mean by "art." For if, when we say "art," we are thinking of Medici prints in the classroom, compulsory attendance at chamber-concerts, or the personal conduction of leg-weary children in a mob round picture galleries, there is only one candid reply. Art, in this sense, is not a necessary element in education at all; it is a "stunt"; a departure, perhaps justifiably pleasant, perhaps merely distracting, and very likely unpleasant as well as distracting, from the legitimate routine of school work. A knowledge of old masters is absolutely necessary to the vocational training of the painter; but I see no reason to suppose it necessary to that universal groundwork of general education which ought to underlie the vocational training of a painter, a barrister, a bishop or a bricklayer.

At this point I can hear accusing voices raised in protest. Certainly, I shall be told, art is not necessary; indeed, I do it wrong, being so majestical, to ask it to submit to the vulgar test of utility. "All art," I shall be reminded, "is quite useless"; and its only justification is its beauty. The very essence of art is its withdrawal from the region of practical affairs into the charmed circle of its own fairyland, its "distance," its aloofness; to raise the question of its utility is to commit the injustice of condemning because it is not practical that whose whole value lies in its remoteness from practice.

Be it so. What follows? A knowledge of art is not a necessity to human life, but it is an ornament, an added grace, lending charm and colour to an existence that would otherwise be sordid, mechanical and dull. The barrister adds beauty to his life by cultivating a taste for Chinese porcelain; the bishop by keeping up his interest in poetry; the bricklayer by going to the Old Vic or hearing classical concerts. Thus art is a relaxation of the practical strain of everyday life, an escape from the all-pervading gloom and squalor of our urban civilisation, a side issue, a backwater of the mind, an ornament upon a fabric whose structure is a matter not of art, but of engineering. Hence the place of art in education is to foster aesthetic tastes which will give us the means of using our leisure in a manner at once agreeable, intelligent and respectable.

Such, I suppose, is the argument that underlies the inclusion of aesthetic elements in education conceived not as essential to it, but as a "stunt," an "extra" which it is amusing to have if you can afford the time and the money. And the theory of art on which this argument is based commands, no doubt, a widespread assent, and betrays itself in countless ways both in our theory and in our practice. The good old theory of school extras— drawing, music, dancing—the latest psychological doctrine of art as "distanced" from real life[1]—the aestheticism which revels in the luxurious conviction of the uselessness of art—the scientists' attack on classical education for its uselessness, and the classicists' defence of it for its freedom from practical concerns, which is the same thing under another name—all these are based on the same profoundly vicious philosophy of art. The error in question, like all errors, contains a grain of truth; and it is because the truth is important that the error has vitality enough to be formidable. The truth is that beauty and utility are not the same thing, and that art as such is not practical life as such. The error is to suppose that, because art as such is not practical life as such, to say what it *is not* throws light on the question what it *is*: to suppose, in other words, that its own proper positive nature is determined by this bare negation, this bare

1. How far that doctrine falls under my criticism depends upon how far "distance" is conceived as *the* characteristic feature of aesthetic experience.

statement of the fact that it is not something else. The result of such an assumption is not merely that art is left undefined, but that we are given a positively misleading account of its nature; for since everything real is sooner or later in some sense useful, we are driven to infer that art is nothing real, and to bestow on it a kind of residual or marginal existence, feeding on the crumbs that fall from the table of utility. Clean design is useful, therefore (on this view) it cannot be beautiful; and if a building is to be beautiful it must be made so by smearing it over with totally useless ornament. A well-trained scientific intellect has nothing to do with beauty; so if education is to develop the sense of beauty, it must (on this view) do so by adding to a scientific training an accretion of aesthetic exercises which are recognised as being aesthetic for no reason except that they are obviously futile.

Art, so conceived as the bare absence of utility, is a familiar enough object. It is the source of all decoration, in the sense in which decoration is the fundamental vice of all bad artists. Architecture as an art means, in this sense, not the dignity and grace of the naked building, but the prudishness that covers this nudity with irrelevant fig leaves; literature means not the expression of a meaning but the systematic concealment of meanings behind wreaths of artificial flowers of speech; and so forth. And our revolt against this kind of art, our yearning to massacre the whole tribe of artists in this sense of the word "artist," is not a revolt of utility against beauty, but a revolt of beauty against ugliness. We want to sweep away the pattern on the wallpaper because we want to see the wall; to get rid of the stencilled roses on the bedroom jug in order to see the jug; to shear away the flowers of speech in order to hear the statement; because the

wall and the jug and the statement have each a beauty
of its own that cannot be heightened and can only be
spoilt by the addition of ornament.

The fact is that, though utility and beauty are not the
same thing, nothing can be truly useful without thereby
acquiring beauty—a peculiar and unique beauty that
blossoms, as it were, out of the soil of sound design. Hence
to argue that because utility is not beauty, therefore,
whatever is beautiful is useless, is not only a logical
blunder; it is setting a premium on bad design and fostering the superstition that whatever is useful is ugly.
And since education, as a preparation for life, is either
useful or nothing, it follows that art and education cannot conceivably have anything to do with one another,
and that the aesthetic elements in education constitute a
breach or interruption in education's proper task—in
fact, an "extra."

To digress for a moment: the superstition that the
useful must be ugly and the beautiful useless seems to be,
in our time, a relic of the industrial revolution, which
by introducing new methods of manufacture necessitated
new types of design, and introduced these new methods
with such rapidity that the old schools of design failed
to keep touch with them. Hence the old designers retained an out-of-date tradition of manufacture, while the
new manufacturers had to create a new tradition of design, and did it at first very clumsily. The artist and the
manufacturer, who were identical in the days of Phidias
and Leonardo da Vinci, were suddenly torn apart. The
artist ceased to be an efficient manufacturer and the
manufacturer ceased to be a properly-trained artist;
and thus artistic design acquired a false association with
antiquated methods of production and gimcrack or un-
seaworthy products, while mechanical efficiency ac-

quired an equally false association with clumsy and re-
pulsive design. False, because the artist in repudiating
machinery deprived himself of endless new sources of
beauty, and the manufacturer in repudiating artistic design deprived himself to a very great extent of efficiency.
If we are to recover the artistic sanity of the Greeks and
the Middle Ages and the Renaissance, we must first recover the conviction that nothing can be beautifully
made unless it is efficiently made, nothing efficiently
made unless it is beautifully made. For it is artistic sanity,
and nothing else, that is outraged when we try to stop
our children enjoying the terrible beauty of an express
locomotive and bid them admire instead a gloomy old
picture or a still gloomier colour-print that purports to
reproduce it.

To return to our subject. The function of art is not to
add beauty to the unbeautiful. Nothing can do that; if a
thing is ugly, you cannot beautify it by decorating its
surface. You must start again from the beginning; and
when you have designed it well, you will find that it has
"come" beautiful without any decoration. That is what
happens with a racing-yacht or a Roman aqueduct; and
these instances show the falsity of conceiving beauty as
something added, by a process of decoration, to the useful; for they achieve beauty simply by being well designed. What is well designed is, so far, beautiful; and
what is badly designed is, so far, ugly. If we call a house
beautiful when it is uneconomically or inconveniently
designed, we do so by a confusion of thought, because it
reminds us of some other house that really was beautiful,
not because we truly and sincerely find it beautiful in
itself; and if we think a machine ugly when its design is
good, that is because we cannot intuitively recognise or
feel the goodness of its design.

But if all good design is beautiful, and if beauty is the proper object of the aesthetic faculty, everything well designed is a work of art; and the function of art in life is therefore not ornamental, but structural. And if art has an essential place in life as a whole, it must have an essential place in education. But to say this is not to say that all education ought to include a study of Medici prints and classical concerts. To study these things is to practise, not art, but the history of art.

Art is an activity, one of these fundamental forms of mental activity which some philosophers call the categories of the spirit. Art is not a quality of objects (there are, strictly speaking, no *objets d'art*); it is a mode of acting; a necessary mode, in so far as every mind that is a mind at all acts in this way. Our ordinary name for this mode of acting is "imagination." To imagine is to be an artist; to imagine well is to be a good artist; to imagine superlatively well is to be a great artist. And there is no mind that exists without imagining; of that we can be tolerably certain, not only from introspection and observation, but from reflection on what it is to be a mind. To be an artist is to create for oneself a world of imaginary objects whose function is to express to oneself one's own mind. Since the life of art is activity, and creative activity, the testing of ready-made works is at best a subsidiary part of it, and not its heart or core. Thus, to be a musician is not to contemplate the melodies that other musicians have made, but to have in one's soul a running spring of music, a fountain of melody welling up from the depths of one's unknown being and revealing, in the perpetual creation of musical imagery, the mystery of that being. If the musician is a poorly-endowed creature, his creations will merely repeat each other and the music that he has heard; if he is a person of stronger and more original character, they will bear, as we say, the stamp of his own personality and of the unique moment that gave them birth. Similarly, to be a man of letters is not, essentially, to read and enjoy ready-made literature; it is to be perpetually creating a new literature—a poor thing, perhaps, but one's own. To be well educated in a literary sense is not to enjoy Shakespeare; it is to write well and speak well; and by "well" I mean, not ornamentally, but expressively, clearly, lucidly, forcibly. To have one's eye for form and colour well educated is not to enjoy Titian; it is to see in the mind's eye coherently and vividly, whether the object one is trying to see is a human face or the inside of a gear-box or the elevation of a cottage.

The art of literature, then, is the art of speaking one's mind; and speaking one's mind, whether to oneself or to another, is the same act as making up one's mind. The thought that before utterance lies obscure and unrealised in the dark places of the soul, in "the chaos of preordination and the night of its forebeing," comes into living existence in the act of expressing it: a person who has not, somehow and in some kind of language, *said* what he means, does not yet *know* what he means, and strictly cannot be said to *have* a meaning. Thus the act of imagining, which is the act of uttering language, is not an embroidering of a pre-existent thought; it is the birth of thought itself. Speaking or writing is, therefore, at once practising the art of literature and bringing into actuality the thought of one's mind. Reading Shakespeare, on the other hand, is studying the history of literature; the words which we read are only the historical record of Shakespeare's literary activity, and our reading of them, in so far as it is *we* that read them, is a literary activity of our own in which Shakespeare's activity lives again, however distorted or diminished by the difference or inferiority of our own mind relatively to Shakespeare's. But in so far as we are trying not to express ourselves, but to re-express Shakespeare, we are restraining, not stimulating, our own imaginative activity; we are putting our imagination to school, not indulging it in the free play of its powers.

Putting our imagination, I said, to school. And that brings me back to education. The study of art history is not the free play, but the discipline or education, of the artistic faculty. By studying literature we develop our powers of speaking and writing; by studying pictures, our power of imagining and depicting our imaginations. This is the justification of the Medici print in the classroom and the visit to the picture gallery and the study of classical literature. But is it a complete justification? or rather, does it justify the study of Botticelli and not that of posters, the study of Beethoven and not that of music-hall songs? Certainly not. What is wrong with the Medici print habit is not that it implies admiration for Botticelli, which may be all right, but that it implies contempt for posters, which is all wrong. But, I shall be told, Botticelli is good art and the posters are bad art. That may be; but the distinction between good and bad art cuts across the distinction between art that is, and art that is not, useful for the purposes of education. Our traditional classical education is based on Greek literature, not because Greek literature is the best literature, but because it lies in a peculiar way at the roots of modern European civilisation. Perhaps Chinese poetry is better than Greek; but it can never be so relevant to the needs of the modern European pupil. Similarly, the textbooks of history, of mathematics, and so forth, which we put into the hands of the young, are not chosen for that purpose

because they are historical or mathematical masterpieces
—in general they are very much the reverse—but because they are the kind of thing that our pupils need. And
it is matter for serious consideration whether Botticelli
is what our school-children need. If he is, it is futile to
set him before them and expect them to understand him
straight away. You might as well read them Dante in the
original and expect them to understand him without being taught Italian; for to appreciate Botticelli means
learning to sympathise with his technique and outlook
and the society of which he was a product, and this is
just as hard as learning Italian, and requires the same
kind of instruction and application, which may very well,
in many cases, be a waste of time.

Imagination is a fundamental mode of mind's activity,
and the right training of the imagination is therefore a
fundamental part of education. But this does not mean
that all education includes or ought to include a study
of those works of bygone art which we have decided to
call great. It means that all education includes and must
include a training of that creative activity which by
bringing language into existence reveals thought to itself.
Indeed, on closer inquiry we shall find that all education
not only contains an aesthetic or imaginative element,
but is in its very essence aesthetic or imaginative. And
this is a necessity which no teacher and no pupil can
escape, and which no reformer, however fanatical, can
defy. All children have always insisted, and will always
insist, on having their rhymes and songs and tales, their
pictures and tunes and dances; if you don't provide them,
they will make them up for themselves; if you are wise,
you will help them to educate themselves by fostering
this primitive poetic activity, stooping to its level and
feeding it with the poems—spoken poems, sung poems,

painted poems, acted poems—for which it craves. "All education begins in tales, true and untrue; and the untrue come first."

Now all art falls into two great divisions: poetry and prose. This is, roughly, Plato's division between untrue tales and true tales. Poetry is pure imagination; prose is imagination as controlled by and consciously expressive of thought. Poetry first, prose afterwards. That formula contains the true view of art's place in life, as opposed to the false view that prose comes first and that poetry only decorates this pre-existent object. We begin by imagining, and in imagining we discover our thought—a thought that did not actually exist till discovered. Poetry is the "mother-tongue of mankind," the universal form of primitive literature, preceding it in historical evolution at every phase of the world's history. The consciousness that first expresses itself in poetry, in fantasy and myth, afterwards clarifies out and sobers down into prose, into science and philosophy. The progress of thought is a perpetual passage from poetry to prose and a perpetual birth of new thought in the form of poetry.

The distinction between poetry and prose is the key to the distinction between education and life. Education is the preface to life, the preparation for life; and this preface or preparation turns out, on examination, to be made of the stuff of which poetry is made. Just as poetry proceeds by creating imaginary objects and dealing with them according to laws laid down by the imagination for itself, so education proceeds by setting imaginary problems and solving them according to arbitrary rules; and by raising and solving these imaginary problems the pupil learns how to solve the real problems of what is significantly called, as opposed to school, "real" life. Education, as the antithesis of real life, is unreal life, imaginary life, a life in which we imagine ourselves in the world of affairs without really being there or even believing ourselves to be there. It is the essence of school life that the pupil should be engaged upon *experimenta in corpore vili*, that he should not bring disaster upon himself when he fails or involve his rivals in disaster when he succeeds; that his successes and failures should be mimic successes and mimic failures. But this imaginary or mimic life really equips him for the work of real life just because its problems, though only imaginary problems, are problems at which he really works and does not merely imagine himself as working. If he only imagined himself to be working at them, his schooling would do him no good; he would awake from it as from a dream and find the real world as alien and intractable as ever.

Real life, on the other hand, partakes of the nature of prose. For in prose the imagination is still, indeed, awake and active, but it is working under the control of thought. Prose is not prose unless it is beautiful, but its beauty must be achieved not by the free imaginative treatment of an arbitrary problem, but by the lucidity and vividness with which thought solves the necessary problem of expressing to itself the nature of the real world. In real life we are not free to work at whatever strikes the fancy of those responsible for organising our society; our problems are forced upon us by reality itself, which bids us solve them or perish. They are not mimic problems, but real problems. And our solutions of them may certainly be beautiful, but only as the locomotive and the ship are beautiful, with the prose beauty of clean design.

Since the purpose of education is to prepare the pupil for real life, education is a poetry whose function is to pass over into prose. If this seems an unprofitably abstract account of education, a mere empty dialectical formula which, however it may amuse a frivolous philosopher, can do nobody any good, let us look at it from a practical point of view and see what consequences follow when it is so taken. We will consider various arts, and ask ourselves how the above principle applies to them. Let us begin with literature.

Here our principle yields two propositions: first, that literary education ought to proceed by way of poetry; secondly, that its function is to give birth to prose. Its end is to enable the pupil to express his own thoughts clearly and intelligibly, and to understand the expressed thoughts of others. He is to be judged not by his knowledge of books, but by his own literary output: his conversation, his business letters, his memoranda, his instructions to subordinates, and conversely, his ability to read a letter, to listen intelligently, to understand other people's instructions. These things are the prose of literature. Its poetry, which constitutes the means of literary education, is similarly twofold, proceeding by creation and absorption. The pupil must not only read Shakespeare and Milton, but—in reality far more important— hear nursery rhymes and childish stories, read all manner of fiction and of fact read as if it were fiction; simple narrative history, novels, detective stories, and so forth. The teacher's part is to select such fictions as will most helpfully stimulate his imagination, neither feeding him on food too hard for his tender stomach nor putting him off with milk when he is ready for meat, and, above all, not frittering away his strength by introducing him to all manner of works in all manner of styles from all manner of periods irrespective of his own special needs and the special problems of his own age. On the other hand, and this is the more important side, the pupil must be taught to create poetry, not only by writing verse—an exercise that is not even yet sufficiently accepted as a necessary part of elementary education—but by writing prose essays on a theme arbitrarily chosen, which are philosophically, though not metrically, poetry. And here again, the teacher's function is to demand of the pupil precisely that standard of excellence which the pupil at this stage of his career could reasonably demand of himself.

The same principles hold good with respect to the training of the eye. Drawing, painting and modelling here correspond to the creative side of education, and the study of drawings, paintings and modelled objects to the receptive side. And here, too, the distinction between poetry as means and prose as end holds good. There is imaginative drawing pure and simple, like an artist's sketch, and there is drawing whose purpose is to express thought, like an engineer's diagram. The function of this branch of education is to enable the pupil to express himself in prose drawing; to draw a map to show someone where to go, or a face that he wants to remember, or a piece of work that he wants a builder or a smith to execute, and conversely, to understand and use such drawings. But this ability can only come through practice in poetic drawing, the free and imaginative presentation of any form that comes into your head. First, learn to control your medium, to handle pencil and brush; then apply your skill to the problem in hand.

Without a training of this kind no one is properly educated. And this we partly recognise when we insist that everybody who is to be thought educated must read and write; for writing is nothing but a specialised form of drawing, and reading is a similarly specialised interpretation of drawings. But, by a fatal confusion of thought, we separate drawing from writing and assume that, while everyone can write if he takes the trouble, drawing requires a special gift. This is simply an illusion. The same muscular control and training of eye which enable a pupil to write enable him to draw; not, perhaps, as well as Dürer could draw; but that is no reason why he should refuse to draw at all. He might as well refrain from speaking because he is unlikely ever to speak as well as Cicero. The ordinary man needs to speak, to write, to draw, ordinarily well, and no more; but that much he does seriously need. We recognise the possibility and the necessity of this in the case of certain professions and trades that simply cannot be carried on without drawing. In these cases no one would accept the plea that an engineer's or surveyor's drawings are bad because he is one of the people who "can't draw"; for everyone knows that the drawing required in those professions can be learnt by anyone who tries to learn it. But we might extend the principle a little further. Everyone would despise a collector of folk-songs who wrote: "I heard a very interesting tune on this journey, but my secretary, who knows how to write music, was not with me." Yet a world-famous authority on ancient art actually has written: "I cannot give an illustration of this work, for I had no artist with me when I visited it." This means that the authority on ancient art is a man who cannot draw, and the man who makes his drawings is no authority on ancient art; and the result is that the expert's opinions and the artist's drawings are, each in its own way, irremediably damaged. A man can get along without being able to draw, just as he can without being able to read; and hard labour may make the latter a scholar and the former an historian of art. But a scholar who has to depend upon others to read aloud to him is less severely handicapped than an art historian unable to handle the medium which he is studying. And learning to make a decently good drawing is no harder than learning to read.

At the other end of the scale, it is equally discreditable that an artisan should not be able to work from a drawing without somebody at hand to explain the drawing to him; and that any person who wants something made should not be able to supply the maker with a drawing of what he wants; and that anyone whatever should write an illegible hand. "Any man who has the use of his limbs," wrote Lord Chesterfield, "can write any hand he likes," which is perfectly true; but Lord Chesterfield, in his eighteenth century individualism, forgot that the fathers have eaten the sour grapes by which the children's teeth are set on edge, and that to have the use of one's limbs one must be trained in accurate muscular control at an early age. To write badly is certainly a thing to be ashamed of; but the blame lies partly at least with those who have neglected the bad writer's elementary education.

There is room for at least equal improvement with regard to music. Here song is the poetry of which articulate and modulated speech is the prose; and a person badly educated in a musical sense is one who cannot so control the mechanism of speech as to make his voice audible and expressive. The best preparation for speaking is to be had by learning to sing; and all those failures of elocution which mar the utterance of so many speakers are due to errors in the technique of voice-production which are, in the main, easily corrigible by a good singing-master—are, in fact, the faults which in his very first lessons every singing-master sets about to eradicate. Yet these faults are startlingly common even among persons whose profession requires them constantly to speak in public. To take one such profession only—not as especially blameworthy, but as especially a matter of concern to myself who am a member of it—University lecturers are often inaudible to everyone more than a few yards away from them, so that the student who has been advised to attend their lectures comes back to his tutor saying, "I have given up going to So-and-so, because I can't hear a word he says."

The same general principles govern the art of bodily gesture, where the poetry is dancing in all its branches—including every kind of athletic exercise; if anyone doubts that tennis is essentially a dance, let him go to the cinematograph and see a "slow-motion" picture of Mademoiselle Lenglen—and the prose is any work like bayonet-fighting, or throwing bricks out of a cart, which demands rhythm and ease of gesture. The Greeks were quite right to regard military drill as a kind of dance; and athletic exercises in general are, as the Greeks knew, an indispensable part of all education.

These notes must suffice to show that our conception of aesthetic education is no mere theory, but a principle that may powerfully help in the work both of understanding education as it is and of creating education as it ought to be. Developed along the lines suggested above, it leads to some such educational programme as this. Education in the arts, which is the only education that can be regarded as truly universal, ought to begin—where in point of fact it always has begun—in the nursery, as soon as a child becomes educable, which means, as soon as it has acquired the regular physiological habits whose establishment is the first care of mother and nurse; and it should form the main contents of what we call elementary schooling. The child should learn to speak fluently and clearly, not necessarily in the standard English of literary circles, but in the dialect of its native place; for the attempt to eradicate local peculiarities of grammar and pronunciation is only a waste of precious time in the pursuit of a motiveless and unattainable uniformity. It does not matter what speech is learnt, so long as it is rendered flexible and expressive by exercise upon topics of all kinds. The child should learn, at the same time, to sing correctly and sweetly, and to do rhythmic exercises, giving it the fullest possible control of its limbs. Reading and writing should be learnt concurrently with drawing, and experience suggests that the normal child can cover the elements of this ground very adequately by the time it is eight or nine years old. For some years after that I believe that its time will be best spent in deepening its knowledge and perfecting its skill in the arts already begun, reading fiction and poetry and historical narratives, practising itself in writing and drawing, speaking and singing, and athletic exercises; and only when a solid foundation has been laid in this way do I think that the normal child should begin to study science seriously; though no doubt mathematics and some elementary science may begin earlier.

These and other details of time-table and curriculum must be left to discussion among experts in elementary education. My aim is not to usurp their province, but to suggest principles in the light of which such discussion may profitably go forward. And it can hardly be doubted that the lack of such principles is a serious impediment to intelligent discussion and constructive reform. To these practical ends my purpose is to contribute by stating a theory of aesthetic education: the doctrine, namely, that the life of mind is a constant movement from poetry to prose, from imagination to thought, and that whereas education as a whole is poetry as contrasted with the prose of real life, so elementary education is poetic poetry or aesthetic education as contrasted with the prosaic poetry of advanced or scientific education. If this main principle is sound, it will follow that the earliest education of a child ought to aim exclusively at training the imagination by the practice of all the arts; but this practice (and here comes in the work of the teacher) must always take a form appropriate to the child's stage of development. Small children will often take keen delight in old masters and in classical music; but experience confirms what on *à priori* grounds we should expect, that these things are not their normal nutriment; and a flight of imagination in which they rise to the level of the Waldstein Sonata is only an interval between periods in which their minds react, perhaps disconcertingly, to the tune of "It ain't going to rain no more." For this reason, while clearly recognising the paramount importance of art in education, we must avoid forcing on the child's attention those objects which its elders, no doubt rightly, consider to be great works of art, and school ourselves to realise that drawing trains and singing nursery rhymes are, on the whole, better and more fruitful means of aesthetic education than looking at Tintoret or listening to Bach. Above all, we must get rid of the idea that the aim of aesthetic education is to impart an ornamental culture to our pupils, and realise that a right training in art is the absolute bedrock of all sane human life.

‏➤➤➤➤➤➤➤➤➤➤➤‹‹‹‹‹‹‹‹‹‹‹‹‹‹‹‹‹‹‹‹‹

Form and Content in Art

E VEN the best of artists are human, and therefore capable of turning out bad work. The father of poets has set his children the example of nodding, and small blame to his children if in this, as in other matters, they have followed where Homer led. Critics, that hardy and self-sacrificing race of beings who voluntarily incur the enmity of artists for the sake of the common welfare, have to classify the various manners and causes of nodding in poets. I do not claim to be a critic, but I want to call your attention to a particular kind of nodding which presents a curious problem in the theory of art. I will call it the nod of the uncongenial subject.

Captain Marryat may provide an example. I do not think him a novelist of the highest rank, but I do think him, at his best, a definitely good one. A great deal of

Reprinted from *Journal of Philosophical Studies*, IV (1929), 332-345.

AUTHOR'S NOTE: This paper forms the text of a lecture given to the British Institute of Philosophical Studies in February 1929. In printing it in the Institute's own *Journal*, I have allowed the style and construction of the original lecture to stand unaltered, adding a few comments in the form of footnotes.

his work is shamelessly derived from the best eighteenth-century models, Fielding, Smollett, Sterne, and so forth; but there are occasions on which he seems to forget all this, and to rise on his own wings into the authentic air of fiction. The incident of the boatswain's trousers in *Midshipman Easy*, the description of the life of a Greenwich mudlark in *Poor Jack*, the portrait of Mr. Chucks in *Peter Simple*—these may not be great work, but they are good work, the work of a man who sees his subject clearly and can find words to describe it tellingly and tersely. But when you turn to *Masterman Ready* or the *Children of the New Forest*, all this has disappeared. The clear vision has gone, the pointed description has gone, the firm economical writing has gone, and you are left with a mere welter of sloppy stuff expressed in fumbling language.

There is nothing strange about this. Marryat was a sailor; he knew the sea and loved the service, and had thought a certain amount about it; at any rate, he had watched sailors for years together, and understood them thoroughly. When he sat down to write about them, his head was full of ideas, and the ideas brought the words. If Marryat had had no literary gift at all, his experience of sailors would not have produced that effect, and he would have written badly even about the things he knew well. If, on the contrary, he had been a real literary genius, he might have been able to endow the virtuous Mr. Seagrave with the same life that he bestowed on Mr. Thomas Saunders. As it was, he was a half-and-half writer, neither a perfect fool nor a perfect genius, and very naturally his work was half-and-half too. It is all very simple. But what I want to point out is the relation between choice of subject and quality of work. Marryat somehow becomes a good writer when he writes about the sea, and a bad one when he writes about anything else.

This is a very common type of case, and it affects writers of bigger calibre than Marryat. Thomas Hardy, for instance, who seems incapable of doing poor work when he is describing the life of agricultural labourers in his own country, becomes a pretentious and almost incompetent magazine story-writer when he tries to deal with fine ladies. And it is not confined to literature. Turner, who could draw a line-of-battle ship out of his head with every rope in its right place, became an ordinary bungler when he tried to draw a human figure. So, if Marryat nods over an uncongenial subject, he nods in distinguished company.

But, after all, why not? Must not the artist be stimulated or inspired by his subject? Is it not right and proper, and in the very nature of art, that the artist should enjoy the full use of his powers only when they are excited to activity by an exciting theme?

That suggestion certainly appears to have something in it when we consider cases like those which I have just mentioned. In these cases it is evident that the painter or writer in question was interested in some things and not in others, and that he painted or wrote well when it was these interesting things that he was describing. Yet there are cases which seem to point to a very different conclusion.

Take Jane Austen. The world of village gossip which she depicts was a world which, no doubt, she knew as thoroughly as Marryat knew the Navy. But you cannot find in her work any counterpart to *Masterman Ready* and the *Children of the New Forest*. When she leaves her villages and goes to Bath or Bloomsbury she does not leave her style behind. She seems, in a sense, indifferent to her subject. She writes about village life because that is ready to hand; something she must have to cut her teeth on, so she cuts them on the Bennet family; but one feels that any other subject would have done as well, or at least that she knew her job too thoroughly to attempt anything that she could not do.

The contrast between Marryat and Jane Austen, I think, may be put by saying that Captain Marryat was a sailor who wrote books, and Miss Austen a writer who lived in a village. I do not mean that Marryat was a worse writer than Jane Austen. As a matter of fact, he was; but that is not the point. I should say equally of Thomas Hardy—the earlier Thomas Hardy of the Wessex novels—that he was a West-country peasant who wrote books—peasant first and writer afterwards, the second conditioned by the first. Of a Marryat or a Hardy it would be, broadly speaking, true to say that they had to be stimulated to literary activity by the presence of a stimulating subject. Of Jane Austen it would be, broadly speaking, false. She did not fall in love with her themes; they did not excite her; she used them, a trifle cold-bloodedly, as material for the construction of a book.

There seem, in fact, to be two types of artist, characterized by fundamentally different attitudes toward their subject. One type waits on the subject. The subject must come to him and excite him, inspire him, raise his artistic faculties above the pitch of mediocrity, which is all he can achieve when the subject is less exciting to him. The other type takes the initiative. He does not wait for the subject to arouse his faculties; he is a skilled man, the master of a craft, and he chooses a subject for the exhibition of his skill with no more emotion than that with which the surgeon contemplates the case on which he is about to operate.

These two types of artist are generally known as the romantic and the classical. Romantic art lays stress on the interesting or exciting character of its subject; classical art does not. The romantic artist does not expect himself to produce good work except when his emotions are being aroused, or have been aroused, by some experience which is to become the subject-matter of his work; the classical artist does not recognize any such limitation. The romantic artist thinks of artistic success as dependent upon inspiration; the classical artist thinks of it as dependent upon skill.

It ought to be explained that this is not the only sense of the word classical. It is also used in other senses, not always in opposition to romantic. Sometimes "the classics" mean any works universally recognized as great, and in this sense the term classical is applied to thoroughly romantic artists like Beethoven. Sometimes, again, classical art merely means art which imitates admittedly great models, as when one speaks of the classical style in eighteenth-century English architecture. But for the present I am going to ignore these senses of the word, and use it simply as the opposite of romantic. The classical spirit is the spirit of perfect design, craftsmanship, mastery of material and construction; it is the formal spirit, the spirit whose aim is to achieve perfect form, perfect lucidity and expressiveness. The romantic spirit is, by comparison, a thing of incoherence and disorder; it prides itself on having something to say, not on how it says it; it despises formal perfection as a mark of chilliness and lack of inspiration, and it cares little for its touches being in the right place so long as its heart is in the right place.

Classical art, in a word, stands for form; romantic art for content. The romantic artist expects people to ask, What has he got to say? The classical artist expects them to ask, How does he say it? The romantic ideal of art is that the things it says should be notable things, exciting things, things in themselves deserving of utterance; and for the sake of their intrinsic importance it is tolerant of imperfections in the way in which they are expressed. Hence, in the absence of a notable or exciting subject, it lapses into triviality. A romantic poet like Wordsworth is sublime when he writes of sublime things, but when these fail him he becomes merely silly. A romantic painter like Turner, when he fails to impress you with the majesty of his subjects, irritates you by the repetition of a very few technical tricks. The classical ideal, on the other hand, is that whatever the artist says should be said as well as possible. Do not trust to the subject to carry you away and force you to express it clearly; do not waste power in letting the subject overcome the dead weight of your own incompetence; learn your job, and be interested in that, not in your subject. Thus classical art will deal with quite uninteresting subjects, or deal with interesting subjects in a quite uninterested way, and will exasperate the romantic critic by wasting time over dull subjects and not even trying to pretend that they are anything but dull.

Romantics are obviously warm-blooded and excitable people, and they often accuse classical art of being cold and passionless. That is a mistake, but a natural mistake. The classical artist is cold-blooded about his subject, but he is not cold-blooded about his work. The romantic portrait-painter falls in love with his sitter, and hopes that this will make the portrait a good one; the classical portrait-painter does not fall in love with his sitter because he is already in love with his art.

A very able critic, Mr. R. H. Wilenski, has written a book about *The Modern Movement in Art*, in which he has discussed the nature of romantic painting in a way that I can only call brilliant. He has illustrated the romantic character of a great deal of recent painting in an extraordinarily forcible and enlightening way. He shows, for instance, that the romantic artist concentrates his attention on the most exciting features of his subject, and comparatively speaking neglects everything else; thus a romantic portrait-painter like Sargent will emphasize the eyes and mouth of a woman, and paint them with great vigour and skill, but will content himself with a baldly conventional placing of his figure on his canvas and a frankly slovenly treatment of the accessories. The motive force of his picture is the excitement which he feels about the woman as a woman, precisely as Wordsworth writes a poem to express the excitement he feels about a mountain as a mountain. That is romantic art: art whose appeal is derived from the appeal of its subject—emotion recollected in tranquillity.

To the romantic art of the recent past, Mr. Wilenski opposes the architectural art of the modern movement. All really modern painting, he says, is directed to building up a structure of shapes. It is concerned with volumes or masses, and it regards a picture as first and foremost an arrangement of these volumes. This is not only true of cubism, with its artificially geometrical way of emphasizing certain aspects of solidity; it is quite equally true of all genuinely modern movements in painting. And, because it is concerned with the volumes of things, and not with the emotions these things arouse in us, Mr. Wilenski says that the modern movement in art is classical.

This is one of the very few things in his book with which I have the boldness to disagree. And I mention it here because I can find no better way of explaining what I mean by classical art. Classical art, most people would agree, is formal art; and what should this be but the art that attends to the forms, that is the shapes, of things?

To argue like that is to fall a victim to an ambiguity in the word form. It is quite legitimate to use form in the sense of physical shape, and to say that a painter attends to the forms of his subject when he attends to its shapes. But when we speak of formalities and formalism, and of the opposition between form and content, we are not using the word in this sense at all.

This will become clear if for a moment we stop talking about painting[1] and take illustrations from a different art. No one, I think, would allow the question whether Dickens was a classical or a romantic novelist to be decided by appeal to the question whether he had attended to the shape of Mr. Pickwick. And I cannot even suggest how the most misguided critic might apply this criterion to Beethoven, for musical compositions have no physical shape at all, and words like "outline" are used of them only metaphorically.

Yet the distinction between romantic and classical art certainly applies to music. Beethoven is certainly a romantic composer, Mozart certainly a classical one. What do we mean when we call Beethoven romantic? We refer primarily, no doubt, to some unmistakable flavour or colouring in his music; but we must try to analyse this flavour and see what has produced it.

The difficulty of this analysis is to reconcile the peculiar case of music with the suggestion I have already made about the function of the subject in a work of art. I said that romantic art was an art which depended for its value

---

1. Mr. Wilenski expressly declaims any intention of putting forward a general theory of art applicable beyond the special field of painting. But the terms classical art and romantic art are used outside this special field, as well as inside it; and no explanation of their meaning can be ultimately satisfactory unless it is applicable to the whole extent of their usage.

on the memorable or exciting or important nature of its subject. This works well enough in the case of painting, because a painting generally has a subject; and it works in the case of literature for the same reason; but music seems to have no subject at all. I do not, of course, refer to what musicians call a subject. A musical "subject" is part of the musical composition itself. The subject of a work of art, in the sense in which I am using the word, is something distinct from the work, something which the artist is generally said to describe or represent in the work; and in the case of romantic art, it is because the artist has been impressed by this other thing that he proceeds to express himself in the work of art.

Now it is clear that there are certain things about Beethoven which bring him into relation with this definition of romantic art. His music has an air of making weighty assertions, conveying a message, presenting philosophical or prophetic utterances. You remember the character of one of William de Morgan's novels, who at a period of dejection and misery heard someone play the rondo-subject of the Waldstein sonata, and said to himself, "Well, if *that* is so, there can be nothing to worry about." And this is just the comment that would have pleased Beethoven, who did definitely claim not only to be a bit of a philosopher or prophet himself—I do not knew whether he distinguished very accurately between the two characters—but to express his thoughts in his music. And these claims are taken seriously not only by people like Joseph Vance in the novel, but by our latest commentator on Beethoven, Mr. W. J. Turner. I am not too clear about these matters myself. I do not find it easy to say exactly what the message is, which Beethoven so forcibly and impressively lays before us; and I should be sorry if my opinion of Beethoven's music were dependent on my opinion of his competence as a philosopher or his trustworthiness as a prophet. But in spite of that, I recognize that Beethoven himself had no doubts about it, and this fact contributes a definitely romantic element in his music.

There is another romantic element about Beethoven in the fact—again vouched for by himself—that he never composed without, as he put it, having a picture before him. The Pastoral Symphony he describes as "expression of feelings rather than painting"; but they are feelings derived from the contemplation of nature, and therefore we can identify the subject of that symphony and say that the relation between it and its subject is a romantic relation. And this brings us to the question of programme-music, which is all explicitly romantic in character, whether its subject is *Les Barricades mystérieuses* or *Harold in Italy* or *Le Boeuf sur le Toit*. And talking of Couperin and Berlioz and Monsieur Darius Milhaud, it always seems to me curious that the French, who most loudly defend the classical ideal, should be the most impenitent perpetrators of programme-music.

Musical critics, in attacking and defending programme-music, have often been distracted by a quite unimportant side-issue: the value or justification of a detailed "programme" in the sense of a document in words telling the audience what the music is about—in schoolboy language, a crib. They have not always realized that to call a piece of music by a title at all, as opposed to a mere descriptive reference-number like "String Quartet in C♯ minor, opus 120," is in principle to make it programme-music, to attach it to a subject and so deprive it of the proud epithet absolute. Nor have they always faced the question how many musical compositions which now have no title might have had a title if the composer had chosen to reveal it in one way or another—in the way, for instance, in which Beethoven said of the opening of the Fifth Symphony, "that is how Fate knocks at the door."[2] When these questions are faced, it can no longer be fancied that programme-music is an innovation of the nineteenth century, a freak of Berlioz and Richard Strauss and a handful of other eccentrics, to be attacked or defended as such; it must be recognized that programme-music is simply romantic music, one of the two great divisions into which music, like all the arts, has always fallen. Beethoven's programmes, we have seen, consist partly of philosophical ideas, partly of imagery drawn from natural scenes. This combination is quite typical of his generation, and brings him into close connexion with men like Wordsworth, Coleridge, and even (if we may accept Ruskin's interpretation) Turner—in fact, with all the romantic nature-worship and nature-philosophy so characteristic of the late eighteenth and early nineteenth centuries.

We can now return to the case of modern painting. It is claimed that this is a classical movement because it is concerned not with feelings but with volumes and masses. But to select a subject for a picture because it has volume and mass, or because it shows an interesting arrange-

2. It is relevant to point out that even unauthorized titles like "The Moonlight Sonata" attached by the public to works of Beethoven have their significance. They show that the romantic flavour of the music is widely recognized, and its significance in the main correctly apprehended by its hearers. People do not, as a rule, feel called upon to attach romantic titles of this kind to works of Mozart, but to works of Beethoven they do; and this fact is not accounted for by postulating in the hearers a strong "visualizing" faculty or the like. A person who knows his way about in music begins "visualizing" when the music asks him to begin; or rather, he begins, not *visualizing* (for that implies a concentration on one kind of sensuous material), but building up in his mind *some* kind of non-musical "subject" for the music to which he is listening.

ment of volumes and masses, is to select a subject for its own intrinsic qualities, and to trust to these qualities for the success of the picture. It is to throw the responsibility for the picture upon the subject instead of the painter. And that is the very definition of romanticism.

It makes no difference whether the exciting thing about a woman is her femininity or her volumes. If her femininity inspires an Academy portrait, and that is rightly called romantic art, the picture of her volumes, exhibited at the Salon des Indépendants, has exactly the same reason for being called romantic. Similarly, if the cloying harmonies of Victorian musicians were romantic because they were intended to suggest a maiden's prayer, the breathless dissonances of our modern composers are every bit as romantic because they are intended to suggest an express locomotive. The composers might wince to be reminded of the fact, but it is Romance that brings the 9.15 into their works. Classical art, I must repeat, does not mind what its subject is. It does not say to itself "We must avoid this, because it is in Dickens; we must avoid that, because it is the sort of thing Academicians paint; and we must choose the other because it gives us a feeling of modernity or proletarianism or emancipation from conventional standards." To choose subjects in that spirit is to label oneself a hopeless and incorrigible romantic. To rebel against romanticism will never make anybody a classic; indeed, the deliberate anti-romantic is only a romantic with an inferiority complex.

Do not suppose that I am an enemy of modern art. I am nothing so foolish. As a matter of fact, I enjoy much of it heartily, and my private opinion is that it is an improvement on the art of the last generation. I would rather see women painted with their faces all corners than with the exaggerated softness and fluffiness that are still the con-

ventional marks of a female portrait. But that is not because I think angularity classical and fluffiness romantic.
It is because I am tired of fluffiness and welcome a little
angularity for a change. I do not think Cézanne was a
great man because he emphasized volumes; I think emphasizing volumes is a good thing because Cézanne did it;
and when a sufficient number of imitative duffers have
done it, I do not promise never to look back with a sigh of
regret to the chocolate-box Academy portraits of my
youth.

My argument hitherto seems to have led to the conclusion that practically all artists are romantics, and that
there are no classical ones except Mozart and Jane
Austen. I will not spend time in asking whether any
others could be found, or whether these too could be
tarred with the brush of romanticism if we tried hard
enough. But I want to raise two questions, which cannot
be discussed satisfactorily except in conjunction. First,
is romantic art worse than classical art? Secondly, was our
initial separation of them not too drastic?

Mr. Wilenski's discussion certainly implies that classical art is the best kind and romantic art an inferior
kind. There is something to be said for this. An artist
who can only work well when inspired by a peculiar kind
of subject is obviously not so skilled, not so much master
of himself and his craft, as one who is free of that necessity. Yet it may not be thought certain that skill and
mastery of a craft are the essentials of a great artist. It may
not unreasonably be said that the greatness of an artist
ought to be judged by the work he has done, not by the
question whether he could have done it as well in the
absence of an inspiring subject. If that is so, the necessary
superiority of the classical artist disappears.

But, it may be replied, romantic art always has a tendency to suffer for its neglect of technical perfection by becoming incoherent and disorderly and allowing speech to be replaced by bluster, music by mere noise. That is true; but when it is good art it succeeds in keeping this tendency at arm's length. It does not always succumb to it; if it did, then romantic art would be a synonym for bad art, or rather for no art at all. Good romantic art does succeed in expressing itself; it does achieve technical success, and is therefore not inferior to classical art.

But this is only because it is partly at least identical with classical art. Classical art is that which achieves technical perfection, that which, whatever it says, says it as well as it can be said. It follows that every artist who succeeds in producing a work of art at all is, to some extent, a classical artist. A merely romantic artist would be a person whose inspiration was only expressed—if this can be called being expressed—in rantings and mouthings and meaningless gestures. It is the classical element in his art that keeps him out of that morass and makes him able to create something that really expresses him.

Art may therefore be at once romantic and classical. In deriving inspiration from its subject, it may be romantic; in converting that inspiration into expressive form, it must be classical. In this sense all art is classical.

But in order that it should be entirely classical, more than that is needed. We said that the classical artist is rather cold-blooded about his subject, and does not fall in love with it. We cannot, surely, say that this is true of all art, after saying that the opposite is true of romantic art.

This is not so certain as it may appear. You may be passionately interested in a thing at one moment and not at another. For instance, you may begin doing a piece of work because you very much want to earn some money;

and suddenly, in the middle of the work, you may find that you have forgotten about the money and are only interested, for the moment, in the work. Or again, a painter may begin painting a lady because he is in love with her; but in such cases painters have been known to get into trouble because, once absorbed in their work, they have been discovered looking at their model not with the eyes of a lover but with those of an artist. For the moment the lover has ceased to be a lover; his love for the woman has given way to absorption in the task of painting. He may have been a romantic artist when he began to paint, but the work of painting, of its own accord, turned him into a classical artist before he had done.

The romantic and classical attitudes are quite compatible, when they are looked at as phases in the rhythm of artistic creation. The artist begins by being interested in a subject for its own sake; he likes it, or fears it, or feels that he understands it, or wishes to understand it better; he is taken by its shape or its colour or its softness or hardness; he feels drawn to it or repelled from it by instinctive impulses. These interests he takes as the subject of a projected work of art. At this phase the only value of the work of art lies in the fact that it is to express his interest, and if this interest had no importance the work of art would have none. But now begins the actual labour of artistic creation. The germ of this process is the original interest; but more than the germ is needed if the process is ever to reach its conclusion. The original interest must not die, but it must be subordinated to the literary or musical work, the painting or carving, that is going to express it. In the first phase the artist is a romantic. But unless he stops being a romantic and becomes a classic, the original interest in the subject will absorb all his attention, and he will never get to work with his pen or his brush. Thus Beethoven may have thought, when that four-note phrase came into his mind, "Fate knocking at the door"; and he may have said to himself, "I will write a symphony about Fate, all full of remorselessness and terror." But while he was scoring the symphony for a full orchestra he did not actually experience terror, he did not uninterruptedly feel the remorselessness of Fate; he was engaged in laying out patterns of sound for a very complicated instrument, and this work, this designing of his score, simply could not be carried out in a condition of terror. Like all very hard work, it was accompanied by a whole *obbligato* of emotions—irritations, apprehensions, triumphs, despairs—but these were concerned not with Fate but with the symphony. In other words, Beethoven was writing music, and writing it in the only way in which it can be written—classically.

The same analysis applies to the simplest water-colour sketch by the most elementary amateur. You see a hill curved against a grey sky; it looks forlorn and sombre, and you paint it to express that feeling. But after you have been painting for half an hour the forlornness and sombreness are no longer in the foreground of your mind; they are taken for granted, and what you are actually thinking is whether your sky is dry enough yet to paint the tree over it. The problems occupying your mind are the technical problems of your craft, that is, you are for the time being a classical artist.

All art, then, is classical art. It is only this classical element that enables the work of art as such to come into existence. The work of art is the creature of the artist's formal or formative power, his technical proficiency; and if anyone objects to this on the score that artists are born and not made, the reply is that, if that is true, it means not that technical proficiency is unnecessary to them, but that they cannot acquire it except on a basis of natural gifts.

But at the same time all art is romantic art. A classical art that was not romantic would be an art with perfect form and no content, perfect mastery of its materials and no subject-matter, a perfectly expressive language with nothing to express. This is not a kind of art or a psychological type of artist; it is a false abstraction. But it is a false abstraction into which people really fall. Molière was caricaturing such a theory of art when he said that everything beautiful and true was in the dictionary—it was only a question of transposing the words. People who talk about music without understanding it have fallen into the same fallacy, and added that all possible tunes have by now been invented; only, unlike Molière, they did not mean it for a joke. Statements like these are based on assuming that art consists merely of patterns, formal arrangements of a given material. So far as it is classical, art is certainly that. But it is also an attempt to express something, to give outward and visible form to the way in which we are impressed by the things we come across in the course of our experience.

The romantic ideal insists on the connexions that bind art to the rest of life. It is romantic in Beethoven to be not only a musician, but also a lover of nature and a bit of a philosopher. It was romantic in nineteenth-century painters to try to be photographers, as Mr. Wilenski shows they did; and I may add that it is romantic in twentieth-century artists to try to be geometricians and engineers. If you could sever these connexions, you would get a sterilized art whose technical skill would never have a chance of showing itself. Now in this sense Jane Austen's art is certainly romantic. We know that she delighted in the society which she depicted, and that she was keenly alive to the pleasures of village gossip. Where she

differed from her neighbours was not in being superior
to these pleasures, but in making them the subject of
works of art. And in this sense Mozart's music also has
its romantic element. It may not offer us profound
thoughts about human character and destiny with such
explicitness as Beethoven's; but no one who is acquainted
with the G minor Symphony or the score of *Don
Giovanni* can fail to see that his works contain a dramatic
or tragic element comparable to that which gives Beethoven his romantic character. To take a single significant
detail: a recent writer has blamed Mozart for the way-
ward, loosely-knit, thematically illogical structure of the
aria *Voi che sapete.* This amounts to saying that here
Mozart is not allowing his work to be determined by
classical principles. The observation is correct. But the
answer—and the writer whom I quote has already stated
it—is that the structure of the aria is perfectly adapted to
the character of Cherubino, who sings it. Mozart is char-
acterizing Cherubino in the same way in which Jane
Austen characterizes Miss Bates.

The classical ideal insists that these connexions between art and the rest of life shall not be so close as to
prevent its being art. The work of art must be itself; it
must stand on its own feet and explain itself in an articulate and intelligible way. After all, the artist's business
is to speak, and his expression is not achieved unless it
is clear, and in need of no explanation beyond itself.[3]

3. Here lies the explanation of the practice of giving titles to works
of art. Of titles given to musical compositions I have spoken above; but
of titles generally, this may be said: that the title is a reference to something not explained by the work of art itself, not explicitly present in
it. As such, it has two functions, one classical and one romantic; and
in point of fact, though emphasis falls now on one function and now on
the other, these functions actually coexist in every case. If a work of art
were purely classical, it would be so completely self-explanatory that a

Good romantic art is art that is well begun. Good classical art is art that is well done. It is always easier to begin well than to end well, and therefore it is easier to satisfy the romantic ideal than the classical. It is a comparatively simple matter to be impressed by something and to feel that you have something important to say. It is harder to discover the best possible way of saying it, and thus make it really intelligible to yourself and other people. What makes this so hard is that you have to subordinate your content to your form; you have to stop being filled with a sense of the importance of your message, and begin attending to the arrangement and lay-out of your exposition. A strong emotion may be the first step towards a poem; but unless you can master the emotion and actually cease to feel it while you devise ways of expressing it, you will never get as far as writing the poem. This was what Wordsworth meant when he spoke of emotion recollected in tranquillity. The emotion is the romantic element, the tranquillity the classical. Yet Wordsworth, after all, was not classical enough; and the defect of his poetry is reflected in his definition of poetry, where he betrays the fact that he sees nothing in the classical, the genuinely

---

title would be unnecessary except for purposes of reference; and "Œdipus at Colonus" may be used for these purposes as easily as "Book iii, ode 3." The classical title, then, merely *labels* a work; the romantic title ("Ulysses deriding Polyphemus" or "Stanzas written in dejection near Naples") *explains* it. Now, if the romantic element in art is overlooked, or regarded as a mere defect, romantic titles will be regarded as a confession of failure, an attempt to evade the consequences of the artist's inability to express himself. But if the romantic element is properly understood, the romantic title appears in its true light, as an indication of the *dynamic* character of the work which bears it. This work is not merely a formal and expressive whole: it has grown out of some germ, some impression received in the course of experience; and the romantic title, telling us what this starting-point was, puts us in a position to reconstruct the work of art for ourselves more easily than we could otherwise have done.

creative, element, except the mere absence of emotion; and even this is not correct, because the labour of composition has its own emotions.

In practice, therefore, it is too often true that to call a work of art romantic is to call it bad. Romanticism by itself never made an artist; and the mere fact that it is the first step in the creation of a work of art means that the artist is in danger of resting there, of being content with the consciousness of a sincere interest in his subject and a genuine desire to produce a work of art. Here modern artists are in the same boat with all artists of every period. There is at present a certain group of subjects which, for one reason or another, have imposed themselves on the minds of most artists. That is as it should be; no one can altogether escape the spirit of his age. But the danger of modern art is the old danger of mistaking correctness in choice of subject for artistic merit. There is no merit whatever in painting a group of people with cylindrical arms and legs, or in writing a novel in which everybody suffers from devastating complexes. The merit lies in getting your cylindrical arms and legs to form a harmonious and expressive arrangement, or getting your complexes to fall into an orderly and coherent pattern. That is what the good artists of to-day are doing. They are not content with being romantically interested in cylinders and complexes, they are trying to subordinate these materials to the formal demands of the classical ideal. The bad artists, now as always, are merely romantic, and think that the intrinsic splendidness of cylinders and complexes will atone for any lack of technical training and artistic talent. And, as the public on the whole agrees with them, and as the critics on the whole follow suit, it is difficult to blame them.

The upshot is that two things are necessary to a work of art: conviction and technique. Conviction, a sense of having something to say, is the romantic requirement, without which a work of art becomes a school exercise or a pot-boiler. Technique, the mastery of the craft, is the classical requirement, without which a work of art becomes an incoherent jumble of random gestures. Where you find a defect of conviction on the one hand or of technique on the other, you have found a defect for which nothing can compensate. Excellence of matter is no excuse for clumsiness of form; elegance of form no excuse for poverty in matter. But in practice the problem which is popularly supposed to arise when conviction outruns technique or technique conviction—the problem of estimating the true aesthetic value of works in which one of the factors seriously outweighs the other—seldom really arises. A defect on the one side is, as a rule, accompanied by a parallel defect on the other. Thus occurs what I have called the nod of the uncongenial subject. It is when an artist has nothing to say that he forgets how to speak effectively. But conversely, until he has learnt to speak, he has nothing to say. He may have feelings working within him, but they are only obscure emotional perturbations, and do not take the shape of a "message," a conviction to be imparted to others or brought clearly before himself. Conviction and technique, the message and the language, content and form, are not two ingredients capable of existing separately and then being brought together into a work of art. They exist together, or not at all.

In saying that every work of art must have these two elements in it, that an artist must have something to say which he feels to be worth saying, and also that he must be able to say it well, I am not asserting anything new. But at least I have some confidence that it is true; and it is so often forgotten that perhaps you will pardon me for saying it again.

MIDLAND BOOKS

MB-1	OVID'S METAMORPHOSES *translated by Rolfe Humphries* (cloth $4.95)	$1.95
MB-2	OVID'S THE ART OF LOVE *translated by Rolfe Humphries*	$1.85
MB-3	THE LOVE ETHIC OF D. H. LAWRENCE *by Mark Spilka, foreword by Frieda Lawrence Ravagli*	$1.75
MB-4	SANTAYANA AND THE SENSE OF BEAUTY *by Willard Arnett, with a preface by Irwin Edman*	$1.85
MB-5	THE EXAMINED LIFE *by Warner Fite*	$1.95
MB-6	THE DIPLOMACY OF THE AMERICAN REVOLUTION *by Samuel Flagg Bemis*	$1.95
MB-7	THE LITERARY SYMBOL *by William York Tindall*	$1.75
MB-8	GEOFFREY CHAUCER *by John Livingston Lowes*	$1.95
MB-9	THE EMPEROR'S CLOTHES *by Kathleen Nott*	$1.75
MB-10	IN THE SPIRIT OF WILLIAM JAMES *by Ralph Barton Perry*	$1.50
MB-11	SKETCH FOR A SELF-PORTRAIT *by Bernard Berenson* (illustrated)	$1.50
MB-12	THE DOUBLE *by F. M. Dostoyevsky*	$1.75
MB-13	PAUL GAUGUIN'S INTIMATE JOURNALS *translated and edited by Van Wyck Brooks* (52 illustrations) (cloth $3.95)	$1.95
MB-14	AFRICAN NOTEBOOK *by Albert Schweitzer* (illustrated) (cloth $3.95)	$1.60
MB-15	THE MORAL DECISION *by Edmond Cahn* (cloth $5.00)	$2.25
MB-16	FORMS OF MODERN FICTION *edited by William Van O'Connor*	$1.75
MB-17	FIVE MASTERS: A STUDY IN THE MUTATIONS OF THE NOVEL *by Joseph Wood Krutch*	$1.75
MB-19	THE ESTHETIC BASIS OF GREEK ART *by Rhys Carpenter* (illustrated) (cloth $3.50)	$1.75
MB-20	THE SATIRES OF JUVENAL *translated by Rolfe Humphries* (cloth $3.75)	$1.65
MB-21	FREEDOM AND CIVILIZATION *by Bronislaw Malinowski*	$2.25
MB-22	JOHN DRYDEN: A STUDY OF HIS POETRY *by Mark Van Doren*	$1.75
MB-23	THE MANAGERIAL REVOLUTION *by James Burnham*	$1.95
MB-24	AGE OF SURREALISM *by Wallace Fowlie* (illustrated)	$1.75
MB-25	COLERIDGE ON IMAGINATION *by I. A. Richards, with comments by Kathleen Coburn*	$1.75
MB-26	JAMES JOYCE AND THE MAKING OF ULYSSES *by Frank Budgen, introduction by Hugh Kenner* (illustrated)	$1.95
MB-27	THE LIFE OF SCIENCE *by George Sarton, introduction by Conway Zirkle*	$1.50
MB-28	OUR AMERICAN WEATHER *by George H. T. Kimble* (illustrated)	$1.95
MB-29	THE THREE WORLDS OF ALBERT SCHWEITZER *by Robert Payne*	$1.75
MB-30	OXFORD LECTURES ON POETRY *by A. C. Bradley*	$2.45
MB-31	ASPECTS OF FORM *edited by Lancelot Law Whyte* (110 illustrations)	$1.95
MB-32	ART AND INDUSTRY *by Herbert Read* (138 illustrations)	$1.95
MB-33	THE TALES OF RABBI NACHMAN *by Martin Buber, translated by Maurice Friedman*	$1.95
MB-34	MAGIC AND SCHIZOPHRENIA *by Géza Róheim* (cloth $5.00)	$2.25
MB-35	THE HISTORY OF SCIENCE AND THE NEW HUMANISM *by George Sarton*	$1.95

(continued on next page)

MB-36	THE GOLDEN ASS by Apuleius, translated by Jack Lindsay	$1.85
MB-37	MUSIC IN AMERICAN LIFE by Jacques Barzun	$1.75
MB-38	DANTE'S LA VITA NUOVA translated by Mark Musa	$1.65
MB-39	NEHRU ON WORLD HISTORY condensed by Saul K. Padover from Glimpses of World History by Jawaharlal Nehru	$2.45
MB-40	THE DISCOVERY OF LANGUAGE: LINGUISTIC SCIENCE IN THE NINETEENTH CENTURY by Holger Pedersen, tr. by John Webster Spargo (illustrated) (cloth $6.50)	$2.95
MB-41	THE PARADOX OF TRAGEDY by D. D. Raphael (cloth $3.00)	$1.45
MB-42	AN INTRODUCTION TO THE GREEK THEATRE by Peter D. Arnott (illustrated)	$2.45
MB-43	REFLECTIONS ON THE DEATH OF A PORCUPINE by D. H. Lawrence	$1.95
MB-44	THE THREE WORLDS OF BORIS PASTERNAK by Robert Payne (illustrated)	$1.95
MB-45	VERGIL'S AENEID translated, with an introduction and notes by L. R. Lind (cloth $5.75)	$1.95
MB-46	ESSAYS ON THE ODYSSEY: SELECTED MODERN CRITICISM edited by Charles H. Taylor, Jr. (cloth $6.00)	$1.95
MB-47	THE LIVING THOUGHTS OF KIERKEGAARD presented by W. H. Auden	$1.95
MB-48	THE QUESTION OF JEAN-JACQUES ROUSSEAU by Ernst Cassirer, translated and edited by Peter Gay	$1.65
MB-49	THE NEW APOLOGISTS FOR POETRY by Murray Krieger	$2.25
MB-50	SPEECH: ITS FUNCTION AND DEVELOPMENT by Grace Andrus de Laguna (cloth $6.50)	$2.95
MB-51	ARIOSTO'S ORLANDO FURIOSO: SELECTIONS FROM SIR JOHN HARINGTON'S TRANSLATION edited by Rudolf Gottfried (illustrated) (cloth $6.50)	$2.95
MB-52	THE ENCHIRIDION OF ERASMUS translated with an introduction by Raymond Himelick (cloth $6.00)	$2.45
MB-53	MARTIAL: SELECTED EPIGRAMS translated by Rolfe Humphries, introduction by Palmer Bovie (illustrated) (cloth $5.00)	$1.95
MB-54	THE IDIOM OF POETRY by Frederick A. Pottle	$1.95
MB-55	THE SENSE OF INJUSTICE by Edmond Cahn	$1.75
MB-56	MANKIND, NATION AND INDIVIDUAL FROM A LINGUISTIC POINT OF VIEW by Otto Jespersen (cloth $4.50)	$1.95
MB-57	D. H. LAWRENCE: THE FAILURE AND THE TRIUMPH OF ART by Eliseo Vivas	$2.25
MB-58	THE CHALLENGE OF EXISTENTIALISM by John Wild (cloth $6.00)	$1.95
MB-59	THE JOURNALS OF JEAN COCTEAU edited and translated with an introduction by Wallace Fowlie (illustrated)	$1.95
MB-60	THREE GREEK PLAYS FOR THE THEATRE translated by Peter D. Arnott (cloth $5.00)	$1.95
MB-61	THE AMERICAN NEGRO by Melville J. Herskovits	$1.65
MB-62	THE CHINESE EYE: AN INTERPRETATION OF CHINESE PAINTING by Chiang Yee (illustrated)	$2.45
MB-63	PERSPECTIVES BY INCONGRUITY by Kenneth Burke, edited by Stanley Edgar Hyman (MB-63 and 64 comb. cloth $6.95)	$2.45
MB-64	TERMS FOR ORDER by Kenneth Burke, edited by Stanley Edgar Hyman (MB-63 and 64 comb. cloth $6.95)	$2.45
MB-65	EARLY MEDIEVAL ART by Ernst Kitzinger (48 plates)	$1.95
MB-66	THE RAMPAGING FRONTIER by Thomas D. Clark (cloth $6.00)	$2.45
MB-67	A STYLE MANUAL FOR STUDENTS: BASED ON THE MLA STYLE SHEET by Edward D. Seeber	$1.25
MB-68	ESSAYS IN THE PHILOSOPHY OF ART by R. G. Collingwood, edited with an introduction by Alan Donagan (cloth $6.00)	$2.45
MB-69	ESSAYS ON DANTE edited by Mark Musa (cloth $6.00)	$2.45